trotman

GW01471501

GETTING INTO

Business &
Management

COURSES

7th Edition

Kate Smith

Getting into Business & Management Courses
This seventh edition published in 2007 by Trotman and Company Ltd
2 The Green, Richmond, Surrey TW9 1PL

Reprinted 2008

© Trotman and Company Limited 2007

Editorial and Publishing Team
Author Kate Smith
Editorial Mina Patria, Editorial Director; Jo Jacomb, Editorial Manager;
Catherine Travers, Managing Editor; Ian Turner, Production Editor
Production Ken Ruskin, Head of Manufacturing and Logistics;
James Rudge, Production Artworker
Sales and Marketing Sarah Lidster, Marketing Manager
Advertising Sarah Talbot, Advertising Manager

British Library Cataloguing in Publication Data
A catalogue record for this book is available from the British Library

ISBN 978 1 84455 114 9

All rights reserved. No part of this publication may be reproduced, stored in a retrieval system
or transmitted in any form or by any means, electronic and mechanical, photocopying, record-
ing or otherwise without prior permission of Trotman and Company Ltd.

Typeset by Ian Turner.
Printed and bound in Great Britain by Athenaeum Press Ltd., Gateshead

CONTENTS

ACKNOWLEDGEMENTS

I am indebted to Fiona Hindle, who wrote the original edition of *Getting into Business & Management Courses*. She is an independent careers consultant, with a background in personnel. Fiona has provided careers consultancy to a variety of businesses and has also written extensively on the legal profession and the City and financial sector. Her clients include major companies as well as individuals of all ages considering career choice. She was a careers adviser at the University of London Careers Service for many years and is experienced in the needs of graduate recruitment. Fiona has also contributed to *Getting into Law*, published in this series.

I would also like to thank Eva Strauss, who made many contributions to this book. Eva works at MPW's London college as Head of Economics and Business Studies and has published a number of books and audio tapes on Economics and Business Studies.

For up-to-date information on business and management, go to www.mpw.co.uk/getintobus

INTRODUCTION

Following a career in business and management is a very popular option for graduates and students choose to do so for a variety of reasons. They gain the opportunity to develop their knowledge of management and domestic and international business through studying a range of companies and organisations and by learning about and gaining practical experience of practical tasks such as business plans, negotiating and giving presentations. The courses are wide-ranging and help students to develop a number of different professional, administrative, communication and technical skills to successfully prepare them for a future job in the field. Graduates with degrees in business and management can go on to such diverse careers as advertising, banking and finance, insurance and teaching.

What do the terms *business* and *management* actually mean and what do these jobs involve? If you are considering working in this field, this guide is designed to help you explore the entry routes and options available in higher education to start you on your career.

WHAT DO BUSINESSES DO?

In its widest sense, a business is an organisation that exists to fulfil the purpose decided by its owners. This definition shows us just how varied and different businesses can be. Usually a business has to make a surplus on its trading (a profit) in order to be able to continue into the following year, but not all business owners see the profit motive as the single most important factor. Firms in leisure and tourism, the music industry or the media are all examples of businesses that are driven by the passions of those involved. Yes, some are also highly successful financially but it would be wrong to say that money was the sole driving force. Even those firms that might be regarded as more mainstream are increasingly aware of the image that they present to the general public and feel that this has to be taken into consideration alongside profits.

Businesses also vary greatly in the size of the company; some are vast public corporations, others small family-run concerns. Many of these multinationals are much larger than some countries. Of the top 100 entities in the world in terms of annual turnover, about half are multinationals and the other half are countries. Working for such large organisations will obviously feel completely different to working for small to medium-sized enterprises (SMEs) employing fewer than 250 people.

Whatever the size of the business, there are also many differing approaches to the best way of running it. Business managers fulfil a variety of tasks and need a whole range of different skills. They need to inspire and give leadership, research, analyse and present information, think laterally in order to come up with imaginative answers, communicate with many different types of people, organise their own time and work to tight deadlines, design complex business strategies and solve conundrums, and to trade off one interest against another. Jobs in business are never dull as the business world is constantly changing and firms are always up against their competitors on the one hand and changing consumer habits on the other. Even very big firms are not immune to failure and decline. The struggling high-street stores Marks & Spencer, WHSmith and Sainsbury's are a good illustration of this. However, these stores, amongst others, have seen a return to their past success recently, with an upturn in profits in 2006. Pressure on many high street stores is now coming from online competitors.

The actual way a business is run in practice is referred to as the corporate culture. This includes all those many things that give the company its character. There are a number of different philosophies on best business practice and a variety of so-called business gurus who write books and run seminars on their ideas. Tom Peters, Peter Drucker and Charles Handy are some of the more famous gurus, but there are also more obscure approaches like *The Zen of Management* or *Pooh for Managers*. Cartoons like Dilbert point out just how often managers get it wrong and how frustrating this is for their subordinates.

DESTINATIONS OF BUSINESS AND MANAGEMENT GRADUATES

Type of work	Proportion
Commercial/industrial/public sector managers	21.5%
Clerical/secretarial	16.8%
Business and finance	15.3%
Marketing/sales/PR/advertising	10.0%
Retail/catering	7.7%
Numerical clerks/cashiers	7.0%
Others	21.7%

The figures are based on those who graduated in 2004. Source: What Do Graduates Do? 2006 *(www.prospects.ac.uk, derived from the Higher Education Statistics Agency First Destination Supplement, HECSU, Graduate Prospects Ltd and AGCAS)*

Employment amongst business and management graduates is good: figures in the 2006 edition of *What Do Graduates Do?* show that about 70% of business/management graduates found employment within six months of graduation, with another 6% entering further education and training and 8.5% were combining work and study.

1

QUALIFICATIONS AND TRAINING

Many graduates pursuing a business career have degrees in the subject but not all fall into this category. Some have studied another subject such as statistics, psychology or English and join a company on its graduate management-training programme. Others have completed vocational courses. It is also possible to become a successful businessperson by working your way up through the ranks from the shop floor – but this is much less common today than it was in the past.

Because managers work in so many different businesses and organisations, and their roles vary from company to company, there is no single route to a career in management. However, you will need certain skills and talents, and a strong academic background will help. The following are academic qualifications that will open up opportunities and help you on your career path.

A LEVELS AND EQUIVALENT

Nearly all A level subjects are acceptable for a business and management degree. A broad selection of subjects would prove a very good grounding for a business career. It is not necessary to take Business Studies at A level, but it's quite common for General Studies to be discounted by some universities. You will need to pay particular attention to each university's entrance requirements. Also note that a modern language A level could be an advantage if you apply for a job with an international company.

You will need to have good grades for the best higher education and employment opportunities. University admissions tutors and subsequently employers will look for good A level and AS level grades as part of their selection criteria. Specific grades will vary but the 'old' universities and the big companies will certainly look for — and get — candidates with mostly grades A and B. A choice of AS level subjects demonstrating breadth — for example a social science, an arts subject, a language and a numerical subject is an advantage.

ACCESS COURSES

A levels need not be the only entry pathway. Many universities now encourage mature students (who may have missed out on the opportunity to enter higher education immediately after school) to apply for entry to degree courses, taking into account their work experience and commitment as part of the entry criteria. There are now Access courses in colleges around the country that specifically prepare mature students for higher education. Mature students make up a growing percentage of the intake of business studies departments, often coming to their degree studies with valuable relevant experience of the workplace.

The main difficulty for mature higher education entrants is that they may not be as accustomed to study as the 18- or 19-year-old entrant. However, they possess an advantage in that they have experienced some of the everyday practical problems they will face in business and management, and they therefore bring important work skills to their studies.

THE DEGREE First degree courses in business studies generally give a broader base than can be gained by studying for a single professional qualification. They provide a foundation in the principles and techniques of modern business and management and the directions in which they are developing. You will be trained in one or more specialist aspects of business studies or management and will have contact with the business world. You will also learn about the sources and uses of information and methods of investigation.

Some courses also cover skills such as accounting, marketing and personnel management. Others give students the chance to specialise in some depth in one of these, or in the management service skills like operational research.

Sandwich courses are usually the more directly vocational and are more frequently offered by the 'new' universities. Nearly all the four-year courses include 12 months' practical training – ie in industry, gaining work experience. The practical training occupies either the whole of the third year – a 'thick' sandwich, or two or more periods of up to six months in different years – a 'thin' sandwich.

Many universities now arrange for placements to be spent working abroad and provide language tuition for students before they depart. A business studies degree is not all taught by conventional lectures and seminars. It also involves extensive project-based work, case studies, business games and other simulations of the business world. So by the time you graduate you are as prepared as possible for work.

POSTGRAD- **DIPLOMA IN MANAGEMENT STUDIES (DMS)**
UATE STUDIES The DMS is a general introduction for non-business studies graduates to business and management, providing an industrial and commercial background and introducing you to management processes, tools and techniques. The course includes quantitative methods, finance, behavioural studies, new technology and management. You would also acquire decision-making and problem-solving skills and learn about the main business functions, including mar-

keting, industrial relations and law. Most courses give students a choice of specialist options. The course is either one year full time or two years part time. You can take this course at numerous universities and colleges throughout the UK, including the London School of Economics.

THE MBA AND OTHER POSTGRADUATE COURSES

The MBA (Master of Business Administration) is a graduate management degree that aims to prepare professionals for management responsibility. MBAs are popular courses which are widely taken across the globe. Deciding on which MBA is right for you is a vital step in your career. In general, MBA courses comprise three elements: a core programme which incorporates lectures and seminars; elective programmes which allow students to focus on their particular areas of interest; and a dissertation or case study. There are many MBA courses available, and students will need to do a significant amount of research before choosing a course in order to find the most suitable one. A good starting point is the Association of MBAs (www.mbaworld.com).

The *Financial Times* compiles a league table of MBA providers, ranked according to a number of criteria including average salaries three years after graduation, salary increase after graduation, career progress, international mobility, and feedback from graduates about the achievement of their aims. Details can be found on www.ft.com.

The 2006 table placed the University of Pennsylvania's Wharton Business School first, with Harvard Business School in second place. The highest placed European business schools were the London Business School ranked in fifth place and Inséad in France in ninth place. Oxford University's Said Business School took 20th place and the Judge Institute, part of Cambridge University, was in 35th place.

But do be aware that having an MBA is not a guarantee of a glittering career. And it is not something you should really consider until you have gained some relevant experience after graduating. In fact, most of the most highly respected business schools will not consider applicants without a minimum of two years' relevant management experience.

In addition to the MBA, there are numerous other Master's courses in business and management, as well as PhDs, and the range is constantly increasing. Courses are available to both business and non-business graduates and may often be more appropriate to take immediately after graduation than an MBA. These include MSc Business and Financial Management, MSc International Business, MSc Management with Marketing and MSc Information and Administrative Management.

THE GRADUATE MANAGEMENT ADMISSION TEST (GMAT)

The GMAT is a test that provides business schools with further information to use to be able to assess the qualifications of applicants for postgraduate study in business and management. Schools use it as one predictor of academic performance in an MBA programme or in other graduate management programmes. The exam does not test specific business-related knowledge or skills but looks at more general academic skills such as verbal, mathematical and analytical writing. To gain more information on what the course requires, reasons for taking it and sample assessment material, please refer to www.mba.com.

FUNDING

Gaining a postgraduate qualification can take time and costs a lot of money. Fees alone are expensive and that is not taking into account the costs of living and accommodation.

You may be able to secure financial assistance for your postgraduate training from one or more of these sources:

■ Local authority grants – Contact your local authority for information.

■ Charities and grant-making trusts — Refer to the books *The Charities Digest* and *The Directory of Grant-Making Trusts 2005 / 2006*, and write to the ones that match your criteria.

■ Career development loans — These are operated on behalf of the Department for Education and Skills (DfES) by a number of high-street banks. For a free booklet on career development loans and for more information call 0800 585505 or visit www.direct.gov.uk/cdl, or for Northern Ireland www.studentfinanceni.co.uk.

■ Bank loans — A number of banks offer loans at favourable rates. The high-street clearing banks are all after your custom as a future potential high earner. So most of them will offer you some kind of incentive to get you to open an account, often with the promise of an interest-free loan. The offers are constantly changing but it is well worth your while shopping around the different banks and picking up their leaflets to get the best deal.

EMPLOYERS' TRAINING

The most sought-after jobs are with companies that run high-quality training schemes. And for an increasing number of companies, these fast-track trainees are recruited from among graduates. Because so many people go straight on to university after A levels, many employers stopped recruiting managerial trainees with only A levels or their equivalent several years ago. So, you are best to start out with the highest possible educational qualifications. This means excellent A levels and AS levels (grades A and B) or equivalent, and a minimum 2.1 degree for the top employers.

For a new graduate, the quality of training often ranks above salary, benefits or the chance to travel when considering an offer of employment. Top schemes have advantages in terms of high-level training, plus salary and accelerated promotion prospects, but they are not for everyone. One limitation is that they tend to be run by the bigger established firms, not the smaller, sometimes more flexible companies. If you opt to apply for such a training scheme, you will find that they are highly competitive. Companies invest substantial amounts of money in training their junior managers in the hope that they will reach the highest levels of the organisation, so they are looking for the best.

But what should you look for? Choosing your future employer requires you to think about your own personal preferences regarding the industry sector and geographical location you want to work in. You might also wish to consider other benefits offered by the company, such as the chance to travel and work overseas. The working environment, especially being around like-minded colleagues, is also worth thinking about. Do you want to be with a group of colleagues of a similar age to you all starting off on a training scheme together, rather like starting your degree? Or would you prefer a more mixed working environment? Once you have thought about these considerations, you then need to look at what management training schemes are being offered by the employers.

It is important that you do your research and find the right scheme with the right company. You will find the names and addresses of employers that run graduate management training schemes, such as the Boots Company plc and United Biscuits (UK) Ltd, in directories like *GET* and *Prospects*.

Because the competition to gain a place on a fast-track scheme with a large blue-chip company is so fierce, many new graduates are forced, and some choose, to look at other alternatives. One option is to work your way up into a general management career via a specialist function, such as finance. One graduate I talked to did not get as good a degree as he hoped and did not manage to secure his sought-after place on a graduate programme. However, he did get a job offer from a large company he had done some work experience with during his summer holidays. They knew his skills and were willing to take him on as a finance assistant. He took the job and made the most of all opportunities that came his way, working hard to demonstrate his commitment. This paid off: the company was delighted with his progress and enthusiasm and within a year transferred him on to a fast-track scheme.

Not all companies have a centralised graduate programme and it is quite possible to find a vacancy in a department, even in a junior role, and work your way up the career ladder. By joining a smaller organisation you will often get an excellent insight into how the whole business operates. And if there are no promotion opportunities within that organisation, you will be able to successfully take your skills elsewhere. So, remember to be flexible when looking at employers. By all means, apply for the 'blue chips' if you think you are in with a chance. But do not overlook the wealth of opportunities available to you within smaller organisations.

CASE STUDY

Graham started six months ago as a graduate trainee on the general management training programme of a large insurance company. He applied to about ten companies through his university's milkround (ie graduate recruitment) programme and was successful at gaining interviews from five of them. He graduated with a 2.1 degree in Mathematics and Management. He did not complete a work placement as part of his course but he had worked during his summer vacations in various retail companies and had also done some temporary office and admin work in a year off before university.

'The competition to get on to the scheme was intense and we all really had to jump through hoops to secure our places. This started with a fairly straightforward one-to-one interview with the graduate recruitment manager on my university campus. I had prepared well for the interview and had done my research on the company, including looking at their website, and I think this really helped and it certainly gave me confidence. I'd also had a mock interview at my careers service which was extremely useful.

'The next stage was an all-day event at the employer's premises. I was with about eight other candidates and we went through a combination of individual interviews with more senior staff and

some group exercises, where they gave us a hypothetical problem and asked us as a group to discuss it and come up with some recommendations. I guess it didn't matter too much what our ideas were, as long as they made some sense, but I think what they were really looking for was to see how we interacted with each other. That included how we communicated our ideas, but also how we listened to others and took their ideas on board.

'We were also given a 30-minute numeracy test where we were not allowed to use a calculator – so remember to brush up on your tables! I must have passed all those tests as I was then offered a place on the scheme to start the following September.

'The last six months have flown by. In the first few weeks all the new trainees received a general induction to the company. There are about 25 of us and that initial induction was great as it helped us to get to know each other. We were all in the same situation, being new to the world of full-time work.

'I have been given my own mentor to give me advice and help with any problems. So far nothing major has cropped up, but it is a big support to know that there is someone there I can talk to if necessary. At the end of my first year I will have a more formal review to discuss my progress. I've also been on some technical and IT training courses. I'm really enjoying the challenge and I'm determined to go as far in this industry as possible and have set my sights on the possibility of an MBA in the future.'

SKILLS AND QUALITIES

A degree, even a very good one, is not enough to get on to a prestigious management training scheme with a notable company. Graduate recruiters are not usually bothered about your particular degree subject – but they will often want their management trainees to be numerate. Subjects such as Marketing, Mathematics or Statistics, Economics, Finance or Business Studies can give you an edge, but some employers still prefer the traditional academic subjects such as history or classics, even for marketing consumer products. However, there are no degree subjects that completely preclude a graduate from entry to a management training scheme.

If you have a good academic background, it will be your personal qualities that will often win you the job. Most companies' recruitment brochures will give you a fairly comprehensive list of skills and qualities they are looking for. Here are some of them:

- Communication skills (these are paramount)
- The ability to think logically and clearly and to analyse accurately
- The ability to research facts and to be able to assess what information is important
- Absorption of, assessment of the importance of and seeing the implications of lots of very detailed information
- Organisational ability
- The ability to work with anyone at any level and get the best out of them
- Building and maintaining working relationships, and summing up people accurately
- The ability to cooperate and contribute to a team.
- Numeracy
- Self-confidence
- Sound business awareness
- Natural authority and leadership
- The ability to think strategically, see the whole picture and conceptualise
- The ability to keep targets in focus and make sure they are reached
- The ability to motivate others, recognise their potential and delegate responsibility
- High ethical standards
- The ability to prioritise information and tasks.

2

CHOOSING YOUR COURSE

You should remember that a degree in business or management studies is not always a prerequisite for a specific job, nor is it a guarantee of a high-flying job. However, a course in business studies provides an excellent foundation and may give you a head start into the world of business over other graduates. Some courses are biased towards particular areas – such as marketing or personnel. If you already have an interest in a particular area of business, look for courses where this interest will be drawn out and developed.

You should also note that about 40% of vacancies advertised for graduates do not ask for a specific degree subject. Many potential employers are more interested in the class of a degree than its subject. If you do want to get into business but do not want to take business studies it should not matter that much – as long as you do well in what you do and end up with a minimum 2.1 degree. But if you are set on studying business or management at degree level, read on, because there are a huge number of courses available and you will need to do some serious planning.

WHAT TO CONSIDER

The basic factors to consider when choosing your degree course are:

- The kind of business and management course you are looking for
- Where you want to study
- Your academic ability.

Going to university is an investment for your future and you need to squeeze the most out of your time there, so it pays to think hard about these points. They are all essential in helping you through the lengthy task of selecting what to study and where. From the huge number of institutions offering business and management courses, it is advisable to start by narrowing down the options to between 10 and 20. Once you have eliminated the bulk of the institutions and courses on offer, carry out your own detailed research:

- Contact your chosen universities or colleges and ask for their prospectuses (both official and alternative) and departmental brochures (if they exist) for more details. Remember that the universities' publications are promotional and may be selective about the information they provide.
- Visit the websites of the universities you are considering. These websites often contain more up-to-date information than the prospectuses.
- Attend university open days if you can, and talk to former or current students. Try to imagine if you would be happy living for three or four years in that environment and address issues such as whether you prefer to be on a campus or in a city and whether there are facilities for you to pursue your other interests and hobbies.
- Talk to any people in business you know and ask for their views on the reputations of different universities and courses.
- Find out what academic criteria they are looking for and be realistic about the grades you are expecting. Your teachers at school or college will be able to advise you on this.

- Make sure the course allows you to select any particular options you are interested in by thoroughly checking out what is available. The list can sometimes be mind-boggling! You will not always know what each option actually covers by its title, so read the department's own prospectus carefully and address any unanswered questions by contacting the admissions tutors direct.

- Think about whether or not you would like a course that includes an industrial placement. This can give you extremely valuable experience and is a great opportunity to make useful contacts for the future. Employers also like graduates who have had a practical placement. It you do choose such a course, it is well worth your while checking whose responsibility it is to find you a placement. Does the university have a placement officer who will help you with this process, or is it entirely up to you to find something?

- Do you want to spend some time abroad? If you are doing a course that has some foreign language content, it may be possible to do a work placement in that country. This could be particularly valuable, as not only would you gain practical work experience, but you would also improve your language skills, which could give you the edge when you come to look for a job after you graduate.

- What are the computer and library facilities like at the university and the department you are applying to? If you do not have your own computer, how many terminals are available for the number of students that are likely to be using them? This can be very important when you are rushing to finish an important project report. You should also check on how readily available are the books you require for the course. Remember, business and management books can be very expensive to buy.

- Try to find out the reputation of the academic staff. If you are going to be taking a business and management degree you might prefer to be taught by academics that have some experience of business themselves. Use the internet to find out what their experience is and what they have published.

Once you have done this thorough research you should have a shortlist of universities that fulfil your criteria – the course that suits your needs, the location, the ability to pursue your interests. From that you can choose the top six places to put down in the UCAS application.

CASE STUDY

Karolina is a third year Business Studies undergraduate. 'My path to reading Business Studies at university started at sixth form college, where I was studying A levels in Biology, Economics and Politics. I enjoyed the independence I was given at college and the way I had to learn to become responsible for my own learning as I felt that this would stand me in good stead for university. Studying Economics at A level and having to read business related articles in the newspapers and relevant magazines meant that I started gaining an interest in the more practical elements of Business Studies. I supplemented my interest with further reading and some work experience at a local telecommunications company. Although I did not have any responsibility at this stage, I shadowed a few members of staff, and observed many business practices.

'I then made the decision to study Business Studies at university and started researching my courses. It was hard to distinguish the courses that would best suit me from the huge number available but I looked at websites to find out exactly what the individual courses would entail and what options were available. I also thought very seriously about the location of the institution itself as I would have to live there for at least three years. I knew that I wanted to be in a town rather than the countryside, but did not want a big city. I was looking to really experience university life. I also wanted to ensure that the course would have a placement year so that I could get some hands-on business experience during my course.

'I got into my first choice and have had a fantastic two years, building my social life as well as working hard at my studies. I am now in my third year and on my industrial placement. I have secured a job in the marketing department of a blue-chip company and have my own role and am responsible for many projects. I hope I have the opportunity to work with them again once I graduate, but appreciate there is much competition to gain a place on one of their graduate entry schemes. I am very excited about all the future prospects and opportunities and can say that my time at university has been a very positive experience.'

SUGGESTED TIMESCALE

YEAR 12

May/June: Do some serious thinking. Get ideas from friends, relatives, teachers, books etc. If possible, visit some campuses before you go away anywhere during the summer.

June/July: Make a shortlist of your courses.

August: Lay your hands on copies of the official and alternative (student-written) prospectuses, and departmental brochures for extra detail. They can usually be found in school or college libraries, but all the information can also be found by looking at the university websites.

YEAR 13

September: Complete your application online and submit it to UCAS via a referee. It will be accepted from 1 September onwards.

15 October: Deadline for applying for places at Oxford or Cambridge.

November: Universities hold their open days and some-times interviews.

15 January: Deadline for submitting your application to UCAS. (Late applications may be considered, but your chances are limited since some of the places will have already gone.)

April: Universities begin to make their decisions and offers will be sent directly to you.

15 May: You must tell UCAS which offer you have accepted firmly and which one is your back-up. (The deadline is two weeks after the final decision you receive if this falls earlier.)

Spring: Fill out yet more forms – this time for fees and student loans, which you can get from your school, college or local authority.

Summer: Sit your exams and wait for the results. When the A level results are published, UCAS will get in touch and tell you whether your chosen universities have confirmed your conditional offers. Do not be too disappointed if you have not got in at your chosen institution; just get in touch with your school/college or careers office and wait until Clearing begins in mid-August when all remaining places are filled. You will be sent instructions on Clearing automatically, but it is up to you to get hold of the published lists of available places and to contact the universities directly.

For more details about UCAS and filling in your applications read *How to Complete Your UCAS Application*.

CASE STUDY

Susannah was always excellent at maths at school and everyone was encouraging her to study it at university. However, although she loved maths and wanted to pursue it further, she felt that she would like a more vocational element to her degree course. Ideally, she also wanted a course that would give her the opportunity to gain some practical work experience, which she knew would make her more attractive to potential employers.

With this in mind she made her selection and was offered a joint degree in Mathematics and Business Studies. 'Joint degrees are notorious for being hard work because you have two subjects to get to grips with, but I actually found that it suited me to have two subjects, because when I was fed up with one I could start studying the other for a break!

'In my third year I did a placement with one of the major accountancy firms. This allowed me to use my numeracy skills, but most importantly gave me such a good insight into business. I also spent some time in their management consultancy practice, which I thoroughly enjoyed.

'Working for a year was great. I felt like a real business person and coming back to university for my final year was really tough at first. However, I realised that I had to knuckle down to studying as I was in with a chance of getting a first. I concentrated and worked incredibly hard, and I was successful in getting my first class degree. I was thrilled, but in order to achieve it I took the decision not to apply for any graduate jobs during my final year and focus on my degree.

'Having now graduated I am going to take a year out to try different jobs and update my skills. I plan to do a bit of temping in different office environments and I'd also like to go to Spain to learn Spanish, as I think having better foreign language skills will help me. I will see how I feel after I have done all of this, but I am considering management consultancy as a future career, having had a taster during my placement year.'

DIFFERENT COURSES AVAILABLE

WHAT'S IN A NAME?

Before you decide to look only at those institutions offering business and management degrees, remember that identical degree titles at different universities do not always reflect very similar course content. Thanks to the wide range of subjects available within a degree, particularly at institutions that have adopted modular schemes, degree titles can easily disguise the full story. By the same token, degrees in seemingly different subjects can be very similar in terms of units of study. For example, the word *business* tends to be a vague umbrella term. Could you guess the difference between Business Studies, Business Method, Business Policy, Business Administration, Business Decision Analysis and Business Operations? The list goes on ...

Business courses do vary in the amount of mathematics and statistics that will be involved. There are no short cuts that enable you to detect from the title of the course what will actually be involved, so you will have to check with each individual institution. Some courses emphasise the importance of managerial costing and accounting, statistical analysis, risk assessment techniques etc, and these will require students to be very confident with figures. Other courses emphasise the human resource side of running a business, methods of motivating staff and planning specific jobs. Needless to say, these courses require much less numeracy.

Very often the mode of study on business courses is related to specific case studies. This is partly because of the very nature of the subject. There are no hard and fast rules in business and students need to learn how to apply textbook theories to specific situations and how to design business strategies, weigh up the risks involved etc. You should also expect to have to make presentations to others on your course as part of your overall assessment.

For practical reasons this book cannot cover all commerce-related degree courses on offer around the UK and the listing in Chapter 8 limited to courses that specify *Business* or *Management* in the title. A variety of courses have been included to demonstrate the diverse range of business and management courses that are available. If you want to thumb through comprehensive lists of available degree courses refer to the *UCAS Student Handbook* or *Trotman's Green Guides: Business Courses* (see booklist). A good starting point is the search facility on the UCAS website (www.ucas.com). You can begin the search by specifying a general subject area of interest, such as Business Studies, and then narrow down the choices by specifying geographical areas, universities or combinations involving Business Studies and other subjects. The search produces lists of universities and courses and provides links to course descriptions, the universities' websites, and teaching assessments undertaken by the QCA (the Qualifications and Curriculum Authority).

SINGLE OR JOINT HONOURS?

If you are considering a single honours course, bear in mind that a good range of optional subjects might make it even more inviting. You may not want to be stuck with just a handful of choices from which to fill in your timetable after you have put down the core courses. Options may come from a similar field or a completely different discipline. Pinpointing specific subjects that you would like to study within your degree can help narrow your choice of university.

Most business and management courses include the core subjects of finance, economics, law, marketing, management and human resources.

In addition, most offer a range of options in the major areas of business such as marketing, finance, human resources, supply chain management, international business and trade, business strategy and small business management. Taking some relevant options may make you more attractive to a particular employer.

Alternatively, if you want to specialise in one other area, a joint honours degree might be more appealing. Some joint degrees do not require previous knowledge of the second subject. Others, especially those with a European language or a science-based discipline, often specify that candidates must have an A level, AS level or GCSE qualification, or equivalent, in a specific subject. In joint degrees, be wary of courses that have similar titles, such as Business with German, and Business and German. In the first, business is the major subject and German is the minor, but in the second, which is more likely to involve a year abroad, you will probably spend equal time on each subject.

EXEMPTIONS

Are you thinking about going into accountancy, banking or insurance? Most commerce-related degrees contain modules that will give you exemptions from some of the examinations that aspiring professionals are obliged to sit for organisations such as the Chartered Institute of Marketing, the Chartered Institute of Personnel and Development and the various accountancy bodies. If you are concerned about which exemption subjects you can include within your degree, call the universities and ask which of the professional bodies recognise their courses.

Alternatively, you can get in touch with individual professional bodies directly and they will tell you which university courses are officially accredited. Although taking exemptions as part of a degree course can be convenient, it is not disastrous for your career if you do not – but your professional qualifications may take around six extra months to complete.

PLACEMENTS AND OVERSEAS STUDY

Studying abroad and/or completing a work placement could also be factors that affect your degree selection. It is possible to study business and management in dozens of countries across the globe as part of a degree based at a British university. Not all of these courses send you off for a full year though; there are schemes that only last for one term or semester. You do not need to be a linguist either as it is always be possible to study overseas in an English-speaking location such as North America, South Africa, Australia or Malaysia. The availability of student exchanges has increased through programmes such as Erasmus, which encourage universities to provide international opportunities where practical – particularly in Europe. And the popularity of overseas study has encouraged some universities to develop special exchange relationships with universities further afield.

METHODS OF ASSESSMENT AND STUDY

Degrees are usually assessed through a combination of examinations (normally spread over two or three years) and coursework, although individual units may be assessed purely by coursework or dissertation. Methods of studying, such as lectures, seminars, tutorials, practicals, workshops and self-study, tend not to vary much between universities (except for Oxford and Cambridge, where they centre around the one-to-one tutorial system). Some institutions, however, do offer part-time courses and even distance learning for a few of their degrees.

LOCATION

While some students have a clear picture of where they want to study, others are fairly geographically mobile, preferring instead to concentrate on choosing the right degree course and see where they end up. But university life is not going to be solely about academic study. It is truly a growing experience – educationally, socially, culturally – and, besides, three or four years can really drag if you are not happy outside the lecture theatre. Below are an assortment of factors that might have some bearing on where you would like to study. See which ones you think are relevant to you and try to put them in order of importance. Again, the search facility on the UCAS website is a good starting point since you can begin your search by specifying regions within the UK where you would like to study.

ACADEMIC AND CAREER-RELATED FACTORS

EDUCATIONAL FACILITIES

Is there a well-stocked and up-to-date business library nearby or will you have to fight other business and management students for the materials? Check for access to computer terminals if you do not have your own or may not have internet access in your room. If you are taking a joint degree involving sciences or languages, make sure there are facilities for your other subjects as well as science or language laboratories. The facilities available will depend on the budget of an institution and plentiful resources tend to attract better tutors.

QUALITY OF TEACHING

This is difficult to establish without the benefit of an open day, but the Higher Education Funding Council for England, the Higher Education Funding Council for

Wales, the Scottish Funding Council and the Department for Education and Learning of Northern Ireland have done the groundwork for you and assessed the level of teaching across the UK already. Their findings are publicly available – see www.hefce.ac.uk, www.hefce.ac.uk, www.sfc.ac.uk and www.delni.gov.uk. Teaching quality may suffer if seminar or tutorial groups are too large, so try to compare group sizes for the same courses at different institutions.

Type of institution

There are basically three types of degree-awarding institutions: the 'old' universities, the 'new' universities and the colleges of higher education.

The 'old' universities

Traditionally the more academic universities, usually with higher admission requirements, the old universities are well established with good libraries and research facilities. They have a reputation for being resistant to change, but most have introduced modern elements into their degrees such as modular courses, an academic year split into two semesters and programmes like Erasmus.

The 'new' universities

Pre-1992 these were polytechnics, institutes or colleges. They form a separate group because they tend to still hold true to the original polytechnic mission of vocational courses and strong ties with industry, typically through placements and work experience. Because of this there are a number of excellent business and management degree courses at new universities, which are very well regarded and highly competitive to get into. Some are still looked down upon by certain employers because of their generally lower academic entry requirements, but the new universities have a good name for flexible admissions and learning, modern approaches to their degrees and good pastoral care.

Colleges of higher education

These are sometimes specialist institutions which provide excellent facilities in their chosen fields despite their size.

They are sometimes affiliated to universities. This form of franchising means the college buys the right to teach the degree, which the university will award, provided that the course meets the standards set by the university.

ATTRACTIVENESS TO EMPLOYERS

Few employers will openly admit to giving preference to graduates from particular universities. Most are looking for high-quality degrees, often a 2.1 or above, as an indication of strong academic ability. But since students with higher A level grades have tended to go to the old universities, it is unsurprising that a large proportion of successful business people come from traditional university backgrounds.

A bit of research you can do yourself is to find out how past students have fared in the employment market. Ask to look at the university's annual final destinations survey, which should be available from the university's careers service, or the department itself.

DISTANCE LEARNING

The vast majority of students choose to study full time and complete their degrees in the shortest possible period. However, if you are a mature student or it would be more convenient to your circumstances, you might wish to explore the option of distance learning. According to the International Centre for Distance Learning there are approximately 15 business and business-related distance learning degree courses that you can study in the UK. Such courses include the BA in Business Studies at the University of East London, which states that 'students can take a shorter or longer time to complete the degree according to their needs and inclination'. However, students are normally expected to study one or two modules at any one time and take a minimum of three years to complete all 18 units.

The Open University also offers a BA degree course in Business Studies. There are no entry requirements for this degree, but the OU requests that 'you must be suitably prepared for study at undergraduate level'. For further information, take a look at the website for the International Centre for Distance Learning at www-icdl.open.ac.uk.

Non-academic considerations

Finances

The cost of living is not the same across the UK, so will you be able to reach deeper into your pockets for rent or other fundamentals and entertainment if you are living in a big city or in the south?

Friends and family

Do you want to get away from them or stay as close as possible? While there can be advantages, financial at least, to living at home, you may prefer the challenge of looking after yourself and the opportunity to be completely independent. You may have deeply personal reasons for applying to a particular university, but it is not a good idea to go to an institution just because your best friend is studying there.

Accommodation

Do you want to live in halls of residence with other students, or in private housing that you may need to organise yourself and could be a considerable distance from college? Most institutions have an accommodation officer who will help you find a suitable place to live. And many universities will guarantee a room in halls of residence to first year students anyway. But you will probably have to fend for yourself at some stage, so check on the availability of student housing, the cost and how far it is from the university. If your university is nearby, is there any point in moving out of home?

Entertainment

Are you going to be spending much time in, for example, the sports centre, the theatre or student bars? How about university societies – is there one that allows you to indulge your existing hobbies or caters for the ones you have always dreamt of trying?

SITE AND SIZE

Many universities overcome the problems of urban v rural and small v large by locating their campuses on the edge of a major town (eg the University of Nottingham and the University of Kent) and centralising certain facilities and services to ensure safety, convenience and some sense of community, even on the largest and most widespread campus. But some students prefer to feel they are part of the local town or city community, rather than being isolated on an out-of-town site. Note that the bigger single-campus universities may cover a larger area than some of the smaller multi-site institutions. And do not be put off by the expression *multi-site* – individual sites are likely to be self-contained so students do not have to travel to other sites too often.

ACADEMIC ABILITY

For the majority of students, their A level scores will be the deciding criterion for selection. It is important to be realistic about the grades you are heading for: do not be too pessimistic, but do not kid yourself about your 'as yet undiscovered genius'. Talk to your teachers for an accurate picture of your predicted results.

Some places specify particular grades but will still take you on if you get the same point score. So, for example, if you are supposed to get BBB (which amounts to 3 x 100 = 300 points), then any combination which produces 300 points (ie ABC or AAD) may be acceptable. However, you should not assume this.

No institution requires an A level in Business Studies from potential students. Few courses specify subjects they want you to have studied (with the exception of most language joint degrees), although traditional qualifications are welcomed everywhere. Conversely, some universities will not accept A levels like General Studies, or the less traditionally academic ones such as Art. Just about all courses, however, demand English and Mathematics at GCSE (grade C or above) or equivalent.

But beware that institutions demanding 'two A level passes and three other subject passes at GCSE level' as their minimum requirement are likely to receive applications from students with higher grades, so that just holding the minimum entry score is not a guarantee of getting a place. Also note that degree requirements are not necessarily indicative of the standard of the course. They tend to be a reflection of the popularity of the course and of the university where it is offered.

SOURCES OF FINANCE

Studying is expensive. Unfortunately the reality of being a student is that you are likely to have incurred debt by the time you graduate. The latest figures from Spring 2005 show that the 2004 NatWest Money Matters Survey, found that the average graduate debt rose by £4055 from 2003 to £12,180. The findings of this report are similar to the Barclays tenth *Annual Graduate Survey*, published in May 2004. This found that the average graduate debt in 2004 was £12,069, 10% higher than the previous year. Out of all the students surveyed, geographical variation showed that students who attended university in the South West had the highest average debt at £14,802, compared to students in the Midlands, who had the lowest average debt at £11,484. The abolition of maintenance grants and the introduction of tuition fees go some way towards explaining this change.

Today, the size of repayments for your student loan will depend on your earnings after you graduate. For most graduates, the repayments will be collected by employers on behalf of the Inland Revenue, and will not begin until your gross income is over a certain level known as the 'repayment threshold'. The repayment threshold for student loans, before deductions, is currently £15,000 per year.

More detailed and up-to-date information about the arrangements for student loan repayments can be found on the Department for Education and Skills website, www.dfes.gov.uk/studentfinance. The Student Loans Company's website is www.slc.co.uk and its telephone number is 0800 405010.

Some employers offer sponsorship to students on a vocational degree course such as Business and Management

Studies. It is worthwhile enquiring about the availability of any sponsorships by writing directly to personnel departments. Also contact the university department and the careers service as they may have contacts with particular employers favourably disposed to sponsoring students. If you are successful, the deal is usually that you will work for the sponsoring organisation during the vacations. But this can give you excellent experience and, if you perform well, the prospect of a job offer after you graduate. If you are seeking sponsorship, contact employers as early as possible as it is common that applications need to be in well before the UCAS deadline.

3

COMPLETING YOUR UCAS APPLICATION

General advice on filling in your application is given in *How to Complete Your UCAS Application*, updated annually (see booklist). The following advice should help you complete your Personal Statement. This is your opportunity to outline to the university admissions staff your reasons for wanting to study a business and management degree.

YOUR PERSONAL STATEMENT

For 2005 entry, UCAS reported that there were 55,277 applicants for business-related degree courses. Of these, 48,580 were accepted. The most popular courses were Management (about 15,000 applications), Business Studies (10,000) and Accounting (over 6000). Applications from men and women were roughly equal. The number of applicants has risen significantly over the last five years: for 2001 entry, there were 45,606 applicants chasing 42,512 places – fewer candidates and more places! Despite the increased competition, on the face of it, it looks as if a high proportion of those applying were successful. However, competition for places at the higher ranked universities is intense and many candidates, whilst being successful at gaining a place on a business-related degree course, do so either through Clearing or at one of their lower preference universities. Employers hold different courses and institutions in different levels of estimation. You should therefore do all that you can to ensure that your choice of university will stand you in good stead in the future. (For more information on how employers rank universities, you should read *From Learning to Earning* – details of this and other useful resources can be found in Chapter 9.)

Because of the competition for places on highly ranked courses, it is particularly important to ensure that the personal statement section of your UCAS application is carefully constructed, and that your predicted grades are high enough so that your first choice universities are able to consider you. The personal statement of the UCAS application is the only chance you get to recommend yourself as a serious candidate worthy of a place. It is therefore vital that you think very carefully indeed about how to complete it so that it shows you in the best possible light. You must sell yourself to the department and make it hard for them not to take you.

Obviously, there are as many ways of completing your personal statement as there are candidates. There are no set rules, but some recommendations can be made.

ACADEMIC POTENTIAL

Universities are academic institutions and thus you must present yourself as a strong academic bet. The admissions tutor reading your application will want to know all the relevant information about you and will want some answers to the following questions.

- What is the strength of your commitment to academic study?
- Why do you wish to study business or management? (Money, status and family pressure are not good enough reasons!)

■ What precisely it is about business and management that interests you? Give details and examples referring to recent business stories you have followed in the press.

■ What do you hope to get out of three or four years of business academic study?

■ What related material have you recently read and can you explain why it interested you?

■ Which particular branch of business interests you most and why?

■ Which business people have inspired you and for what reasons?

WORK EXPERIENCE

Work experience is very useful as it demonstrates a commitment to the subject outside the classroom. Remember to include any experience, paid or voluntary. If you have had relevant work experience, mention it on your form. Explain concisely what your job entailed and what you got out of the whole experience. Even if you have not been able to get work experience, if you have spoken to anyone in business about their job it is worth mentioning as all this information builds up a picture of someone who is keen and has done some research. Wanting to be the next Richard Branson, Anita Roddick, Alan Sugar or Duncan Bannatyne are not good enough reasons to convince a hardened admissions tutor of your commitment to a business degree! You need to show them that you really do have some business and commercial awareness.

FUTURE PLANS

Any plans you have made for the future should also be included on your form. Be precise. Again this will demonstrate a breadth of interest in the subject. For example, you could say *'I am particularly interested in pursuing a career in business. My enthusiasm was initially sparked off by my active participation in the Student Industrial Society at school, of which I am president. I am also an avid reader of the business pages in the newspaper.'*

OTHER ACTIVITIES AND INTERESTS

At least half of your personal statement should deal with material directly related to your chosen course. But the rest of the page should tell the admissions tutor all about what makes you who you are:

- What travel have you undertaken? What have you gained from the experience?
- What do you read?
- What sporting achievements do you have?
- What music do you like or play?
- Do you hold or have you held any positions of responsibility?

In all these areas give details:

> Last year I went to Paris and visited all the Impressionist galleries there. I relax by reading American short stories — Andre Dubus, Raymond Carver among others. My musical taste is largely focused on opera (I have seen 14 productions of The Magic Flute) and I would like to continue playing the cello in an orchestra at university. I would also enjoy the chance to play in a football team to keep myself fit.

This is much more impressive than just saying:

> Last year I went to France. I like reading and listening to music and sometimes I play football at weekends.

GENERAL TIPS

- Keep a copy of your personal statement so you can remind yourself of all the wonderful things you said about yourself, should you be called for interview!
- Print off a copy of your application to remind yourself what you have said. Before submitting it, also ensure you check your application through very carefully for careless errors which are harder to see on screen.
- If you are planning to do so, state your reasons for applying for deferred entry and your plans for the year before entry. For example you might be hoping to find some relevant business work experience followed by some time spent in Europe to brush up your language skills and knowledge of other cultures.

ONLINE UCAS APPLICATIONS All applications in English now use the web-based Apply system. This system allows you to make your UCAS application on a computer at school, college or home – or even from a remote island during your gap-year; you just need to have internet access. Your application is then sent to UCAS via your referee using the internet.

4

Getting work experience

Getting work experience has become more and more significant in recent years, and in a climate where getting into business and management is so fiercely competitive it is not enough to be only a brilliant academic. The more (ideally relevant) experience you have, the better the chance of succeeding in your initial job applications. Many employers will rate work experience as being almost as important as academic qualifications.

What will you gain from work experience?

■ It will give you a true insight into the business world and whether or not that is what you want to do. Some real experience will be particularly useful if you are trying to weigh up which area of business you would like to go into. For example, are you more analytical or creative? Would you be more suited to a career in finance or marketing?

■ It helps you to make a better transition from education into the world of full-time work.

■ It gives you the opportunity to build up those all-important contacts.

■ It gives you a more impressive CV – and will help you to gain excellent (hopefully!) references, which are important for any future career.

However, it is not that easy getting relevant work experience. Most employers recognise this and do not stipulate that it is essential, although it is preferred. If you cannot get experience in a large business, any work experience that demonstrates use of the skills employers are interested in will be valuable. Communication skills, determination, commercial awareness and IT skills can all be developed in many other sectors of business and commerce.

LOOKING FOR WORK EXPERIENCE

MARKETING YOURSELF

There is no single guaranteed way of succeeding in getting work experience, so try as many as you can think of, and be creative in the process. Here are a few suggestions:

■ Ask your teachers at school/college if they have any contacts in the business world.
■ Use your careers library and speak to your careers officer.
■ Talk to your family and friends and ask them if they can suggest anyone to contact.
■ Make sure everyone you know is aware you are looking for work experience.
■ Send your CV and a covering letter to a variety of businesses local to you (see pages 41–4).
■ Keep up to date by reading the business pages of the 'quality press'.
■ Watch and listen to the business programmes on television and radio.

If you have a contact in a local organisation, try asking to go in for one or two weeks' work experience during the holidays, or even ask for one day's work shadowing to get an insight into what the working environment is like. Whichever route you take, it will almost certainly be on a voluntary basis unless you have specific skills to offer, such as good office and keyboard skills. If that is the case, you could try to get some paid work during the summer or register with an employment agency.

How to apply

It is never too early to start to put together a curriculum vitae (CV). This is a summary of what you have done in your life to date. If you have hardly any work experience, then one page on good quality A4 paper will be sufficient. If you are a mature student with a lot of jobs behind you there is sometimes a case for going on to a second page, but for most young people a brief CV will be appropriate. Here are the main headings to cover:

Name; Contact details; Date of birth; Nationality

These are the basic details to head your CV. Make sure they're right!

Education and qualifications

Start with your present course of study and work back to the beginning of secondary school. No primary schools please! List the qualifications with grades you already have and the ones you intend to sit.

Work experience

Start with the most recent. Do not worry if you have only had a Saturday job at the local shop or a paper round. Put it all down. Employers would rather see that you have done something, and every job will teach you some employment skills such as reliability, retail skills etc.

Skills

List everything you do that could have a commercial application – such as computer skills, software packages used, typing, languages, driving licence and so on.

Interests and positions of responsibility

What do you like to do in your spare time? If you hold or have held any positions of responsibility such as captain of a sports team, been a committee member or head boy or girl at school, put it all down. Do you play an instrument or have a creative hobby? Do you belong to a society or club? All these say something about the person you are.

REFEREES

Usually two: an academic referee, such as a teacher or head of your school, plus someone who knows you well personally, who is not a relative, such as someone you have worked for.

Always highlight your good points on a CV and do not leave gaps. Always account for your time. If something such as illness prevented you from reaching your potential in your exams, point this out in your covering letter. To succeed in business you need to have excellent attention to detail, so make sure your spelling and grammar are perfect!

A SAMPLE CV Lay out your CV clearly and logically, avoiding gaps and including any exams you are studying for as well as those taken. Below is an example.

Lucy Mathilda Johnson

Address	1 Melchester Road, Melchester MC2 3EF		
Telephone	0123 456 7890	**Email**	lmj@melchester.sch.uk
Date of birth	1 January 1989	**Nationality**	British

Education **2000–2007: Melchester High School**
2007: A levels to be taken: Geography, German, Mathematics
2006: AS level: Psychology (B)
2005: GCSEs: English(A), Mathematics (A), Geography (A), German (A), Biology (B), Chemistry (B), History (C), Physics (C)

Work Experience **2005–2007 (Saturdays)**
Sales assistant in busy dry cleaner in centre of York.
August 2006
Two weeks as temporary receptionist in small firm of accountants responsible for answering telephone and general clerical work.
2003–2005 (Saturdays)
Delivering newspapers and magazines throughout my local area.

Skills Modern languages – good written and spoken German.
IT – competent in MS Word and Excel, good keyboard skills.

Positions of Responsibility Captain of school netball team, treasurer for Young Enterprise company.

Interests Netball, swimming, reading, travel and music.

References Available on request.

THE COVERING LETTER

Every CV or application form should always be accompanied by a covering letter. The letter is important because it is usually the first thing a potential employer reads. Here are some tips on structuring and presenting your letter.

- The letter should be on the same A4 plain paper as your CV and it should look like a professional business document. Do not use lined paper and keep it to one side of A4 only.
- Try to find out the name of the person you should send your letter and CV to. It makes a great difference to the reader the more you can personalise your application – but do not be over-familiar. Use their title (*Mr*, *Ms*, *Dr* etc) and last name, not *'Dear Bob'*. (Get a book on business letter writing if you need help with the conventions. For example, if you start the letter *'Dear Mr Brown'* remember you should finish it *'Yours sincerely'*. If you do not know the recipient's name and send it, for example, to the Personnel Manager, begin with *'Dear Sir or Madam'* and finish with *'Yours faithfully'*.)
- The first paragraph should tell the reader why you are contacting them (eg 'I am writing to enquire whether you have any openings for work experience').
- The second paragraph should give them some information to make them interested in you by highlighting your interest in business along with some specific skills you can offer; such as knowledge of word-processing or having a good telephone manner.
- Say in the letter if you know anything about the company and how you found out about it, for example if friends or family work there, or you have read anything in the press recently that was of interest or relevant to your career prospects.
- Employers usually prefer typed letters, unless they specifically request one to be handwritten.

Whether you are applying for a position through an advertisement, or just sending a speculative letter to a local company, you should do plenty of research on the employer. Having some information would help you tailor your CV for that particular company, and it will certainly be impressive if at interview you show some knowledge of how the company works.

If you have an application form to fill in, follow the instructions carefully. Always complete forms neatly, using black ink. If your handwriting can be unclear, make sure that you take your time. You probably will not be asked to submit your CV as well, so always add evidence to the statements in your application forms.

It is imperative that you keep copies of all the letters, CVs and application forms you send off, not just so you can remember who you have applied to, but so that you have something to work from at an interview. You are bound to be asked to elaborate on things you have written about yourself, so do not say you have got a skill or an interest if you cannot back it up.

5

SUCCEEDING AT
INTERVIEW

**ACADEMIC
INTERVIEWS**

Outside Oxford and Cambridge, formal interviews are
rarely part of the admissions process. They are expensive
and time-consuming for both the university and the applicants. However, although academic interviews are rare,
they do occur, so if you are invited to attend for interview, here are some points to bear in mind.

- Remember that if you shine in your interview and
  impress the admissions staff, they may drop their
  grades slightly and make you a lower offer.
- Interviews need not be as daunting as you fear. Interviews are designed to help those asking the questions
  to find out as much about you as they can. It is
  important to make eye-contact and show confident
  body language – and treat the experience positively as
  a chance to put yourself across well rather than as an
  obstacle course designed to catch you out.
- Interviewers are more interested in what you know
  than what you do not. If you are asked a question you
  do not know the answer to, say so. To waffle simply
  wastes time and lets you down. To lie, of course, is
  even worse, especially for anyone hoping to demonstrate integrity and honesty suited to a business
  career.

- Remember your future tutor might be among the people interviewing you. Enthusiasm and a strong commitment to your subject and above all, willingness to learn, are extremely important attitudes to convey.
- An ability to think on your feet is vital ... another prerequisite for a career in business or management. Pre-learned answers never work. Putting forward an answer using examples and factual knowledge to reinforce your points will impress interviewers far more. Essential preparation includes revision of the personal statement section of your UCAS application, so do not include anything in your UCAS application if you are not prepared to speak about it at interview.
- Questions may well be asked on your extracurricular activities. This is often a tactic designed to put you at your ease and to find out about the sort of person you are, therefore your answers should be thorough and enthusiastic.
- At the end of the interview, you will probably be asked if there is anything you would like to ask your interviewer. If there is nothing, then say that your interview has covered all that you had thought of. It is sensible, though, to have one or two questions of a serious kind – to do with the course, the tuition and so on – up your sleeve. But it is not wise to ask anything that you could and should have found out from the prospectus.
- Above all, end on a positive note and remember to smile! Make them remember you when they go through a list of 20 or more candidates at the end of the day.

PREPARATION FOR A BUSINESS AND MANAGEMENT DEGREE INTERVIEW

Preparation for an interview should be an intensification of the work you are already doing outside class for your A level courses. Interviewers will be looking for evidence of an academic interest and commitment that extends beyond the classroom. They will also be looking for an ability to apply the theories and methods that you have been learning in your A level courses to the real world.

NEWSPAPERS AND MAGAZINES

As an A level student, you should already be reading a quality newspaper every weekday and at the weekends. Before your interview it is vital that you are aware of current affairs related to the course for which you are being interviewed. The *Financial Times* will give you a good grasp of business as well as reading the business sections of the other 'broadsheets'. You should also keep up to date with current affairs in general.

Magazines are another important source of comment on current issues and deeper analysis. *The Economist* is a popular example, but you may also find it helpful to pick up the more specialist magazines such as *Business Age*. Reading professionally written articles keeps you well informed of relevant current events and gives you the chance to see how professional writers use the vocabulary and language of business to communicate the news and their views. Magazines such as *Enterprise* and *Human Resources* may also have some articles of interest to you. You do not have to buy all these – visit libraries or use the web regularly to keep up to date with the business press.

TELEVISION AND RADIO

It is also important to watch or listen to the news every day, again paying particular attention to business and economic news. Documentaries and programmes about the economy, business ventures, the politics of business and so on, can be enormously helpful in showing how what you are studying is applied to actual situations and events. *Panorama* is a good example of the sort of television programme it would be useful to watch. *The Apprentice* and *Dragon's Den* can also be very informative.

Radio 4 has its equivalent in *Money Box*, and the *Today* programme in the morning has up-to-the-minute reporting on economic and business developments, often with interviews given by those most closely involved.

It is a good idea to know the names of the chairman of the CBI and the Bank of England, for example, and the names of the country's top business people. You can make a point of listening to what they have to say when they appear on *Question Time* or *Newsnight* on television, or *Any Questions* on the radio.

This advice assumes that you will be taking a single Honours business or management degree, but if you have chosen a joint or combined Honours course, you will have to prepare yourself for questions on those subjects as well.

Essentially, the interview is a chance for you to demonstrate knowledge of, commitment to and enthusiasm for business. The only way to do this is to be extremely well informed. Interviewers will want to know your reasons for wishing to study business. It is important to be aware of the many aspects of business – eg marketing, finance, personnel – and be clear about the differences between the various functions.

THE INTERVIEW

Interview questions are likely to test your knowledge of business and economic events and developments in the real world. Any controversial related topics could well be brought up by interviewers and you should be well informed enough to have an opinion about them from a business point of view.

It is important that your answers are delivered in appropriate language. You will impress interviewers with fluent use of precise technical terms and thus detailed knowledge of the definitions of words and phrases used in business and economics is essential.

You might be asked which part of your A level courses you have most enjoyed. You need to think carefully about this before interview and, if possible, steer the interview in the direction of these topics so that you can display your knowledge.

Future plans and possible careers may also be discussed at interview. You will not be expected to have completely made up your mind about this but, by the same token, you will not be held to what you say at interview after you have left university. Previous work experience is useful and you should be able to recall the precise tasks you carried out during your employment and think about them before interview so that you can answer questions on them fully and well. Questions of this kind will be asked to see if you have an understanding of how business and management theories and methods are actually applied in the world outside school or college.

Interviewers will ask questions with a view to being in a position to form an opinion about the quality of your thought and your ability to negotiate. You may be presented with a real or supposed set of circumstances and then be asked to comment on the business implications of them.

Recent business events are very likely to form a large part of the interview and are all possible as the basis for questions. An ability to see the opposite point of view while maintaining your own will mark you out as a strong business and management degree candidate.

Do not forget that interview skills are greatly improved by practice. Chat through the issues we have discussed with your friends and then arrange for a careers officer, teacher or family friend to give you a mock interview.

WORK EXPERIENCE INTERVIEWS

Most of the above-mentioned tips would equally apply if you are going for an interview for work experience. However, in addition you should also do the following:

- Think through why you want the job, and in particular why you want to work for that organisation.
- Research the employer thoroughly before interview. Look at their brochure and website.
- Plan in advance what you think your key selling points are to the employer and make sure you find an opportunity in the interview to get these across.

■ Prepare a few questions to ask your interviewer at the end. You can demonstrate your preparation here by asking them about something you have read about them recently, if appropriate.

■ Remember a nice firm, confident handshake at the beginning and end of the interview.

In any interview situation it makes a better impression if you arrive in plenty of time for your interview and dress smartly and appropriately (people in business tend to look quite formal). Try to appear confident and enthusiastic in your interview – but listen carefully to the questions you are asked without interrupting and always answer honestly.

POSSIBLE INTERVIEW QUESTIONS

Questions may be straightforward and specific, but they can range to the vague and border on the seemingly irrelevant. Be prepared for more than the obvious, *'Why do you want to study business or management?'* But remember, you wouldn't have been invited for interview unless you were a serious candidate for a place or for a work experience position ... so be confident and let your talents shine through.

Some of the following questions are obviously relevant either to academic or to work experience interviews but many could easily apply to both. Try practising your answers to these:

Question: *Why have you chosen to study business and management?*
Comment: Focus your answer to this question around how your studies and work experience have provided you with the motivation and interest to pursue this subject at university. This is an obvious starting point for your interviewers and they will probably want you to expand on the reasons for choosing your course that you highlighted in your personal statement. Assume that this question will arise and practise your answer to it: ensure that what you say is well-structured and that you do not waffle – try to keep your answer relatively short and certainly no longer than two minutes.

Question: *Why do you want to study at this university?*
Comment: This is another standard opening question and one that you should certainly be prepared for. You could talk about why the location of the university appealed to you, or how you were attracted to it via a personal recommendation. A prime factor that distinguishes one institution from another is the course it offers. You will need to ensure that you have researched the course in some depth to see what is studied and how it is organised and structured.

Question: *Have you visited here before?*
Comment: If you have visited the university or attended an open day previously, this is your opportunity to mention it. Remember that the people conducting your interview will have contributed greatly to their department's open day and will welcome your feedback, but do keep it positive! Talk about it being a useful and informative occasion. Your interviewers will expect you to have done a lot of research into your chosen course and institution, so they will be expecting you to be well-informed. (The university prospectuses and websites are good sources of information.) You do need to show that you are familiar with the particular institution that you are applying to. Answering this question by just saying *'No, but all universities are pretty much the same'* will not improve your chances of getting a place.

Question: *What thoughts do you have on what you would like to do after you graduate?*
Comment: Of course you do not need to know exactly what career you would like to follow at the end of your degree at this stage – but you do need to have some thoughts on the kind of job you might be interested in. A possible answer might be: *'I would like a job that incorporates both my education and my practical skills; something combining my A level education with my working knowledge of customer service operations, entrepreneurial abilities and computer and administrative skills.'* If, on the other hand, you do have a clear idea about what you would like to go into in the future, then talk about this – but remember to justify your reasons.

Question: *How do you think you are doing with your A levels?*
Comment: The interviewer will know your predicted grades so you do not need to give too much information about these, but do state that you are working hard and making good progress. Talk about what topics you are studying at the moment, and if you are doing anything related to business and management. Elaborate on the aspects of the course you like, the skills you have gained and/or coursework projects where relevant. This is a relatively boring question, so take the opportunity to direct the conversation towards subjects that you are confident discussing and which will show you in the strongest light. Topics you would be happy talking about should be prepared in advance.

Question: *What has attracted you to this course in particular?*
Comment: This question, like the second one, enables you to show that you have thoroughly researched the particular course that you are applying for. You should draw on a particular aspect of the course that interests you and explain why. The university's website will generally give a precise breakdown of the core units that will be taught each year as well as the optional modules.

Question: *Tell me about any work experience you have had.*
Comment: This is an important question. Expand on the description of work experience that you gave in your personal statement. Do not just list the things you saw and did – mention how you felt about and reacted to what you were seeing and doing. Did you enjoy it? Was there anything that particularly interested or surprised you? Try to give as personal an account as possible.

Question: *What are the main things you learned from your work experience?*
Comment: This is another standard question which follows on naturally from the preceding one. Talk about the varied nature of your experience. There may have been things that surprised you about the functioning of a business or about new technology that was used. How did it differ from your expectations?

Question: *Have you followed any business cases in the news recently?*

Comment: As an A level student you should be reading a broadsheet newspaper every day. Talk about a recent article you have read and why you found it particularly interesting. This is another standard question that it is vital you prepare in advance. If you try to think of a topic off the top of your head without having given it any serious thought previously, you may find that you are out of your depth if you have to deal with further questions on the subject.

Question: *Have you spoken to any people in business about their work? Have you visited any businesses?*

Comment: Talk about people who work in business and about what they have told you, and why you have found what they said interesting or motivating. When discussing a business that you have visited, give a different example from the one that you talked about with reference to your work experience. Mention what you learned about the workings of this business and what you discovered about the way it operates.

OTHER POSSIBLE QUESTIONS TO THINK ABOUT

- What areas of business are you interested in?
- How does business affect your daily life?
- What achievements in the last five years are you most proud of?
- Tell me about a difficult situation in the past five years that you dealt with badly and explain how you could have handled it better.
- What makes a good business person or manager?
- What do you know about us?
- What are your strengths? Give some examples.
- What are your weaknesses? How do you plan to overcome them?
- I've got no questions but you have got five minutes to convince me you should have a place to study here.

6

CAREER OPPORTUNITIES

How often do you hear someone say 'I'd like to work in business' or 'I'd like to be a manager'? These are not uncommon career aims, but more often than not people do not have a real understanding of what being a business person or manager actually involves. The terms are sometimes used as meaning 'being successful' rather than anything to do with the concept of the work. So, first things first: if you are thinking about a career in business and management you need to find out what management means and what are the typical functions or departments within businesses. Let's take a look ...

THE MANAGEMENT ROLE

Whenever you open a newspaper and look at the jobs section, every second advertisement has the word *manager* in its title. Is this just a ploy to attract applicants or is it that some form of management is integral to many jobs? And if so, what do all these people do? Well, they all do different things, and work for an enormous variety of organisations. Yet at the same time they all have certain responsibilities and tasks in common.

The most straightforward definition of *management* in business terms could be 'the achievement of objectives through other people'. So, the primary difference between managerial and other types of work is that it involves getting other people to do the necessary work rather than doing all the tasks yourself.

Essentially, anyone who manages is responsible and accountable for making sure that whatever department or project they are in charge of runs smoothly and successfully. (Depending on the type of employer, this usually means profitably too!) Now this obviously means that you bask in the glory – and hopefully the profits – when all goes well. But when things go wrong, as they inevitably do at times, the manager is the person who will be taken to task because it is he or she who has the ultimate responsibility for what happens. So you can draw the following conclusions about the role of management in business:

- Every job has some managerial aspects. Even the most junior clerical workers must ensure that others cooperate with them so that they can do their job.
- No job is exclusively managerial. Everyone has to perform some tasks for themselves.
- Management is not just about status or being paid better. Some professionals and other specialists, with no real management responsibilities, are often more senior and have a higher salary than many managers.
- The term management also covers a vast range of other activities, including supervision, organisation, administration and leadership. (The job title *executive* is sometimes used in the same context as *manager*.)

Management is undoubtedly a skill in its own right and is essentially the same in whatever field it is carried out. Good managers are not confined to managing work which they are capable of doing themselves. Indeed, in the higher levels of management it can be an advantage not to have the bias that specialist knowledge can produce.

BEGINNING YOUR CAREER

A number of large companies, like PricewaterhouseCoopers, have graduate training schemes for new graduates. With such companies, training is usually undertaken in house through formal programmes and on-the-job experience, and is sometimes combined with study for a professional qualification. However, lots of graduates start their careers in a small organisation, which may not have any formal training programme. Although this is less structured, it is possible to get a wealth of early experience and responsibility by being thrown in at the deep end, while gaining an excellent overview of how the whole organisation operates.

There is no right or wrong answer regarding whether it is better to join a big or small organisation initially. You should consider how much structure and formal training you want and look for an organisation that will give you what you are looking for. If a firm belongs to the Investors in People government initiative, it will place great emphasis on training and career development. Traditionally people reach a management position after a number ofy of experience in a specialist function, such as sales, marketing, personnel or finance.

Graduates in business and management enter a very wide range of careers. These include accountancy, investment banking, insurance, management consultancy, information technology, marketing, business journalism, the media and the legal profession – to name but a few. The list of options is almost endless, but it must be highlighted that many of the careers and employers recruiting such graduates are increasingly global. (See Chapter 6 for further information on career opportunities.)

Many firms have moved away from the traditional hierarchical structure based on business functions (like production, marketing etc) to one based on project teams. Working in a smaller team like this can be very exciting, as there is often a greater sense of urgency and camaraderie amongst the various members. You need to learn how to reach decisions within a group and realise that everyone is different but this does not mean they do not have important skills to contribute. You also learn that no one is perfect and everyone can make mistakes – including you!

Information technology (IT) really has changed the way we are able to work. Some firms now even consist of 'virtual teams', ie people who work together but do not share an office to do this. They may be scattered geographically and communicate via their mobile phones and the internet. They may only work for that company on a few days every week, doing something else for the rest of their time.

TYPICAL BUSINESS FUNCTIONS

MARKETING

The marketing function in business is to make people aware that a product or service exists, and encourage people to buy it. This often requires identifying the most likely groups of buyers and targeting them in specific ways. TV ads, for example, require considerable planning and market research. Marketing professionals will have researched the product and its rivals and identified how and where they want to place their product in the market in order to maximise sales, or promote brand loyalty, or achieve market penetration etc. They will commission an advertising agency to come up with a suitable advertising campaign and monitor how advertising affects sales. Psychologists are often involved in devising advertising slogans or images that will stick in the mind and which will be recalled or will influence us when we see the product.

Careers in marketing are often varied; many people who have worked in marketing later move on to advertising agencies or to work as publicity consultants. Marketing tends to attract people who are creative and good at thinking up original and innovative ideas. However there are also many jobs in market research that require people who can direct discussion groups, design and conduct surveys and process the statistical evidence. For these jobs it is important to have good numeracy and communication skills.

CASE STUDY

After graduating with a BA in Business Studies, Caroline started her career as a marketing assistant in the marketing department of a pharmaceutical company.

'The team I worked with analysed markets world-wide to find which would be most suitable to promote our new products into. This gave me a lot of practical and wide-ranging experience. The company really believes in investing in staff and I was also sent on numerous training courses in all aspects of marketing techniques, so I had a good mixture of formal training and hands-on experience. After a few years, I decided that although I really loved the job in marketing, I came into contact a lot with the advertising industry – and that was a big attraction.'

So Caroline decided to try to progress her career in this area. 'I'd built up many valuable contacts through my marketing experiences, so talking to people I knew in the advertising industry helped me identify the sort of jobs I could go for, and the companies that had vacancies. Eventually I was successful – I've just been offered a job as an account executive with a major advertising agency!'

SALES

Another aspect of business is sales. This work is increasingly commission only. In other words, if you do not sell anything you do not get paid. On the other hand, if you are good at selling, the rewards can be fantastic.

What you sell will depend on the business you work in. Books, advertising, professional services, time-shares, cars, stocks and shares, ideas, computer software – anything that a business produces needs to be sold. The work may involve travelling as a rep or may be desk-based tele-sales, for example. As a manager you will also be responsible for the sales team, whether it is in house or made up of reps based around the country or abroad.

You can be taught sales techniques as part of a business studies course, but you need a basic aptitude to sell really effectively. If you have natural selling skills, this might be an area to consider. If you are not sure whether a job in sales is for you, your summer vacations could be a useful testing period. There are lots of jobs where you could try out your sales technique!

CASE STUDY

Neil has been working at a large retail outlet as a Department Manager for the past two years. He graduated three years ago with a 2.1 degree in Business Studies from Kingston University and successfully got his job by applying through the university milkround. After taking a year off, which combined temporary work with travelling, he joined the company on its 18-month graduate training programme.

'My training has been excellent and I am still learning all the time,' says Neil. 'I have been on short courses covering topics such as teamwork, negotiating skills, customer service, and management skills. I started my training in the soft furnishings department and am now the Department Manager for the books department. I have been exposed to all aspects of running a department, from working on the shop floor, serving customers to learning about stock-taking and display.

'Each day is totally different – you never know what to expect when dealing with customers. Most are very nice but you do have to be tactful when dealing with tricky situations. You need plenty of stamina and flexibility but the rewards are well worth the hard work when you see the sales figures boosted. And the satisfaction of working with your team is tremendous.'

PERSONNEL

Personnel work, or *human resources*, as it is often called, covers every aspect of a business to do with the people in it. As a personnel officer you would be involved in the recruitment and training of staff, implementing company policies and government legislation affecting employees, and maintaining employee records.

In large companies human resources departments analyse staffing requirements, agree targets and devise selection procedures. They organise staff appraisals and administer training and management development policies, and deal with disciplinary matters as they arise. Personnel departments in some very large organisations will often be split into different functions, such as training and graduate recruitment.

In smaller companies there may only be one or two people who have to cover all personnel issues, and these may be a small part of their whole job function. So if you were to join a small administrative department you might get more of an overview of personnel than in quite a large company, where your training may be more specialised. In small companies, it is also quite common that departmental managers deal with personnel issues such as training and discipline.

Personnel work is often challenging and emotionally demanding. The skills required include objectivity (the ability to see all sides of a problem) a reasonable level of numeracy, organising skills and an understanding of all types of people.

CASE STUDY

Alex graduated with a 2.1 degree in Business Studies. In his final year he took human resources management as one of his major options, having decided he wished to pursue his future career in this area. Despite fierce competition he was successful in being offered a place on a graduate personnel training scheme with a major accountancy firm, which he has recently started.

Alex is convinced that his one year's industrial placement with a bank helped his credibility here. So far, his training has given him a thorough understanding of the firm, and he is now beginning to get involved in some recruitment and selection activities, as well as arranging presentations at various universities. He will shortly be starting the professional qualification for the Chartered Institute of Personnel and Development, which his employer will sponsor. 'I know it will be hard work to combine the demands of work with study,' says Alex, 'but I'm convinced it will be worthwhile and I'm really looking forward to it.'

FINANCE

The financial aspects of a business are commonly regarded as the most important. If there is no cash in the tills and the bank wants the overdraft repaid yesterday – that is trouble. All firms have accounts departments responsible for sending out invoices and chasing debtors, paying suppliers and generally drawing up the company's annual accounts. This is known as financial accounting and is concerned with keeping track of the financial side of the business after the transactions have happened. Financial accounting lets the senior management know how well the business has done in the past year. However, it does not prepare for the future. Planning for the future is called management accounting. Here firms draw up very extensive and detailed budgets for every department so that they can keep a tight control on costs and are therefore less likely to make mistakes in the year ahead. Both types of accounting make extensive use of IT.

Accountancy does not have to be boring and desk-bound. It can be a good way to join a creative team in the media industry or film industry – areas that are often difficult to get into otherwise.

The financial sector covers a wide range of careers and employers. These include banks, building societies, insurance companies and accountancy firms. All of these organisations would be open to recruiting graduates with a degree in business and management, as long as your A level grades (or equivalent) are good enough and you have a good degree, which usually means a minimum 2.1.

For example, all the major clearing banks run graduate training schemes which would give you the opportunity to train and work in many aspects of the bank's function over a period of often around 18 months. This will usually mean moving around the country for your various placements. In the case of the banks, you will normally be encouraged to study for the Institute of Bankers' professional examinations. Once experienced, you may be promoted to, for example, a branch manager. In this role you may be involved with individuals and with corporate clients. As a trainee you might have a spell in a department marketing corporate services and then move into a role as a personal accounts executive.

In addition to their general graduate training schemes, most of the large banks also recruit graduates directly into their computing departments. This does not necessarily require you to have a computer science degree and most of these training schemes are open to graduates from any degree discipline.

Most careers within the financial sector will require you to be meticulously accurate and be good with figures. You will also need to have good interpersonal skills, excellent IT skills and be able to work effectively as part of a team.

Purchasing

Most organisations, including manufacturing and insurance companies, as well as public-sector organisations, require expert purchasers or buyers. For example, each year the National Health Service spends in excess of £4 billion on drugs and sophisticated electronics. And central and local government spend well over £150 billion on supplies.

Purchasing is a term mainly used in industry. *Buying* tends to be used in retailing and other organisations will often use the term *supplies*. But the principles of the job are the same. Purchasing managers are now part of a wider profession known as supply chain management. Purchasing is probably at its most complicated in the manufacturing industry, where products such as cars are assembled from many different components. The purchasing manager may be involved from the start, when the design engineers begin to specify the raw materials and the parts needed, starting to pinpoint suppliers and sorting out any problems on new designs.

Skills required for purchasing include the ability to work well with figures, accuracy and the ability to digest technical and other data quickly and easily, as well as excellent communication skills.

TRANSPORT MANAGEMENT

Transport managers are responsible for the safety and efficiency of passenger or freight services. This might include managing and administering on a day-to-day basis at places such as airports, railway stations, ports and bus or freight depots. Tasks would include scheduling and timetabling. The role of the transport manager would also cover the commercial roles open to all businesses, like finance, marketing and personnel management.

If there is an accident, it is the job of the transport manager to investigate and take any necessary action. A vital task is to ensure that health and safety regulations are enforced.

To be successful in transport management you must be good at organising and planning and enjoy working with figures. It is important that you can remain calm under pressure, but are able to think quickly and logically on your feet. Teamwork and good interpersonal skills are essential.

PROJECT MANAGEMENT

Many firms organise their staff into specific projects instead of according to the traditional functions of marketing, finance, personnel etc. People who work on a specific project will come from a variety of different business backgrounds and be together for the duration of that project. They often work as a team, sharing tasks and responsibility, and are more focused on that one project.

Leading a project as project manager requires great skill but can also be very exhilarating.

Management consultancy

The Institute of Management Consultancy (www.imc.co.uk) defines a management consultant as an independent and qualified person who provides a professional service to business, the public and other undertakings.

Management consultants identify and investigate problems within a company concerned with strategy, policy, markets, organisation, procedures and methods. Generally a team is sent to spend time within the organisation to find out what the problems are. They then come up with a set of recommendations for action by collecting and analysing the facts, but still keeping in mind the broader management and business implications. Finally they discuss and agree on the most appropriate course of action with the client, and may remain within the company for a short period to help the client implement these strategies.

Management consultants are high-fliers – they can be recruited from among top graduates, but they are usually people with business experience. The reason is that if you are going to have any credibility in advising others how to run their businesses, you need real-life understanding of such issues. You will also need to be quite sensitive and tactful and have a good deal of maturity. Excellent numeracy, teamwork and interpersonal skills are all essential, as is a strong academic background (usually meaning at least a 2.1 degree from a prestigious university).

CASE STUDY

Paula joined one of the leading strategy management consulting firms two years ago, following a BSc in Business Administration.

'I chose management consultancy for a number of reasons. The training in business was rigorous and I had to be prepared to work extremely hard. It also gave me the opportunity to meet clients from a huge variety of sectors, which will give me the chance, if I want it later on, to move into industry, having gained an excellent background.

'My first project lasted six months, and I worked closely with three colleagues. I was regularly commuting to the north of England to help analyse and assess why a particular manufacturing company had been consistently dropping profits over a two-year period. After much research it was the job of the team to feed back our findings with a list of recommendations.

'From the beginning I had to get used to presenting my work to colleagues and then to our clients in a clear, logical and persuasive manner. At times, the pressure can be enormous for short periods of time. On average I work 55 hours per week. I have had two short-term overseas projects, one in France and one in Hong Kong. You are really rewarded for the actual work you do and that is a strong motivating factor for me. I can't think of a job I'd rather do!'

LARGE COMPANIES — GENERAL MANAGEMENT

Large companies will often have general managers who are responsible for the general running and operational details of a business. Their role is to liaise with other departments, monitor how members of staff are recruited and make sure that training is kept up to date. The general manager is also responsible for ensuring that profit targets are met, as well as keeping an eye on the marketing and promotional aims of the organisation.

Several large businesses run training schemes for both school-leavers and graduates as management trainees. Most schemes give an initial period of training, often 12–18 months, where you receive placements in a number of departments within the organisation, such as finance, sales and marketing. This is a great opportunity to try out different areas and find out what you like and what you are good at – a bit like a foundation course. At the end of the training period you can decide where you want to specialise.

A number of companies have fast-track management programmes with accelerated training and early responsibility.

SMALL BUSINESSES

Large company management training schemes, especially with 'blue-chip' organisations, are always going to be the most competitive to get into. You will certainly get a good and thorough structured training from them, but you should not overlook the often excellent experience you can gain from a smaller organisation.

You will probably be thrown in at the deep end and you are unlikely to have very specific responsibilities, but you will see at close hand the prizes and pitfalls of a career in business. You will see demonstrated the differences effective marketing makes, and will gain first-hand experience of things like dealing with banks and coping with disgruntled customers – in other words, the reality of working in business.

ENTREPRENEURS

If you have got a good idea, have some experience of constructing cashflow forecasts, and do not fear failure or hard work, setting up your own business could be your route into the world of business. Richard Branson started his empire while still at school, as did Alan Sugar. You could also use Anita Roddick and Terence Conran as your role models, both of whom started international companies from small businesses.

It is more common for someone to set up on their own after gaining their experience in another organisation. If you are thinking of starting your own business, you will need a lot of the skills and business awareness that you can best gain from employment. Added to which, you will need to be innovative and creative, energetic and resilient. You will need to be persistent and prepared to work long hours. You will need to be realistic in your business plans, and able to adapt rapidly to changing circumstances. It can be very fulfilling to be self-employed, but make sure it is for you before choosing this route.

WHAT MAKES A GOOD MANAGER?

Many students are attracted by the thought of a managerial career. It has the advantage of being open to any discipline and work is rewarded on merit — your worth is judged by your performance. A managerial career is not dependent on seniority, and it can offer its own rewards stemming from practical achievement in a job where results can be measured.

MANAGEMENT SKILLS

Managers today have to work in an ever-changing and complex business environment; they need to use an increasing number of analytical methods and techniques. An important skill lies in knowing which techniques to use in a given situation, and how to use them correctly. Here are the main skills you will need to be an effective manager.

LEADERSHIP

Good managers are also leaders. The real challenge of management lies in empowering your team to take charge of a project or goal and together achieve more than they believed they could possibly handle.

DELEGATING

Management involves delegating power and responsibility appropriately, not preventing others from developing by hanging on to everything, but not giving unachievable workloads or having impossible expectations.

GETTING THINGS DONE

Good managers are the people who get things done, and they do this by inspiring and encouraging the people working with them.

TEAMWORK

This plays a huge part in successful management and is the main reason why employers frequently ask candidates about their extracurricular achievements and activities. Playing a sport, taking part in dramatic productions or being involved in a school magazine or university society all show ability to work in a team.

MANAGING YOUR OWN WORK

It is essential that the good manager is effective at managing their own workload well and setting standards for their team. This means setting an example in areas such as good organisation, timekeeping, commitment, personal presentation and honesty.

MANAGING STRESS

Because of the pressures of management, good managers will do whatever they can to avoid the effects of undue stress on their physical and mental health – and therefore their productivity. This means having problem-solving skills – noticing if a stressful situation is developing and affecting a team or its members, and being able to deal with it successfully.

POLITICAL AWARENESS

Every organisation has its own culture and politics. Good managers will be aware of the context in which they work, including the sensitivities of other people and other departments, to be most effective at motivating their teams.

MANAGING FUNCTIONS

The management role is broad ranging and responsibilities can be spread over several business areas or functions. For example:

- Operations – maintaining and improving the delivery of whatever service or product for which they are responsible
- Finance – budgeting and monitoring the use of the resources
- People – motivating those they work with
- Information – communicating effectively with everyone at all levels.

LANGUAGES

Language skills are essential and already more than half of the world's population speaks a second language. It is vital to have a thorough understanding of the language and culture of a country to enable effective communication with others – to cope with the nuances of speech as well as understanding documents such as letters and reports. If you are an English speaker you can get by in Scandinavia, the Netherlands, Germany, much of Central and Eastern Europe and sometimes in France and Belgium without local language skills. (This would not, perhaps, be so easy in Spain or Italy.) But in any situation, you will always be at an advantage if you are able to hold at least a simple conversation in the language of the country you are working in.

WOMEN IN BUSINESS

Women have been making a certain amount of progress over the years in reaching the higher posts on the career ladder. In contrast with the 1970s when there were hardly any women in management, today about 30% of managers are women and this percentage is rising steadily. Women managers tend to be more common in certain sectors – personnel, insurance and pensions, marketing – and much less so in others – manufacturing, research and development, purchasing and contracting. Women also tend to do much better in the new internet-related industries, generally known as e-commerce.

It is always difficult to accurately generalise, but women also often have different leadership styles. They have better interpersonal skills and this makes them better team leaders. However there is still considerable resistance in many firms to having an autocratic female boss.

Overall though, the higher up the ranks you go in a large organisation, the fewer women you tend to find and there is usually only one token woman on the board of directors. Currently women occupy 8.5% of European corporate boardroom seats. Norway has made the greatest advances of all the European Union member states in this area with a legal ruling which ensures that women make up 40% of the board of each company and the rest of Scandinavia is not far behind. The rest of Europe still trails these countries, although the number of companies with at least one woman on the board has increased over the past two years (from 62% to 68%). (*Source: European Professional Women's Network, www.europeanpwn.net*)

This 'glass ceiling', which in effect bars women from higher promotion, has meant that a number of competent women have opted out of working for large companies and decided to start up their own organisations instead. There are now quite a number of very successful companies owned and run by women and a strong support network of professional bodies specifically for women in business.

There are various government proposals currently under consideration to make it easier to balance a job together with childcare arrangements. Two weeks' paid paternity leave has been introduced as well as improved statutory maternity pay (SMP). Employees are also allowed a considerable amount of time off work to attend to family crises. Many employers are finding that offering more flexible working conditions can be a win–win situation benefiting both parties. Women in Management (WiM) is a special interest group set up by the Chartered Management Institute to support women managers. Details can be found on the Chartered Management Institute's website (see Further information).

Of the 41,006 students who were accepted onto business or management courses in 2003, almost 50% were women.

7

CURRENT ISSUES

A growing number of companies are realising that they do have responsibilities beyond merely returning dividends to shareholders. The term *stakeholder* is used to mean all the other people, organisations and the environment that the firm impacts on. Some firms are so concerned with the ethical impact of their products that they monitor all the stakeholders of their suppliers as well as how their product will eventually be disposed of. This is known as the *cradle to grave* approach. *Triple bottom line* is a term used to describe the economic, social and environmental performance of a company.

One business director was noted for saying: 'Every business has an impact on society. The choice is to manage it or not to manage it. And why would anyone choose not to manage it?' Brands have been marketed so successfully that they appear to have a very real personality. This means that consumers choose brands depending on what they feel about these brands and brand management is all about keeping your brand's image reliable, cool or ethical in the minds of your consumers. This is not an easy task and firms will tend to spend large amounts on specialist qualitative research into the opinions of their market.

GlaxoSmithKline, Britain's third largest drug company, was very heavily criticised at the World Trade Organization conference at Seattle for pricing their anti-AIDS drugs so high that poorer countries could not afford them. In contrast, the GlaxoSmithKline African Malaria Partnership awards grants totalling over US$1.5 million for malaria research and aid, and hardly anyone knows about this. This shows that often the problem is as much one of public image as what the company actually does.

Ultimately, decisionsin with companies are taken by the people who manage that company. Sixty-two per cent of firms say that they are likely to be influenced to be more socially active by their own employees. Graduates tend to choose the company they want to work for carefully based on their own perceptions of what that company believes in. This is particularly the case when the economy is on the upturn and there are plenty of jobs for new graduates to choose from.

WORK–LIFE BALANCE

People are increasingly working more flexibly. They may have two or more part-time jobs or may work freelance on a variety of often overlapping projects. Some of this may be done from home, from a laptop abroad or in an office where people *hot-desk* (just come in to use the facilities from any desk that is free). This means that the division between work and leisure is increasingly blurred.

Most EU countries have signed the Social Chapter of the Maastricht Treaty, which forbids firms to ask their employees to work more than 48 hours in any week. There is an increasing amount of medical evidence about the damaging effects of overwork. If you work a 60-hour week you will also tend to be less efficient and make mistakes that might be costly to rectify. In the UK, we tend to work much longer hours than our European counterparts.

GLOBAL-ISATION

The EU Social Chapter which guaranteed that social justice would accompany the liberalisation of the European economy. It laid down provisions for improving standards in such areas as working conditions, employment, social security and trades union rights.

Globalisation means that the marketplace has opened up to such an extent that it is very easy to include the entire world. Communication, transport, raising of finance etc have all become much easier and firms have adapted their business strategies accordingly to improve the way they organise their business. Over half of all the international trade in the world is from one part of a multinational to another in a different country.

The standard wage in China is still something like US$14 per week and firms obviously find it worth their while to build state-of-the-art factories there and ship the goods to their markets in Europe or the US. At first it was only manufacturing jobs that transferred to the Far East – but more recently, India in particular has become a nucleus for service industry jobs like call centres and computer programming. It is obviously impossible for the West to be able to compete against these wage levels and so it has to make the most of those aspects of the business where it still has a competitive advantage – in particular, new business ideas.

Businesses in Europe and the US are developing better and ever more efficient ways of managing their brands. 'Think global, act local' is a slogan that is often used here to mean that despite globalisation, different cultures are still more different than we might think. Unless you have a truly international brand like McDonald's or Coca-Cola, your product may need to be slightly modified for each country.

The West also still has an advantage in technology and innovation, but it is not always easy persuading people to continue paying for this *intellectual property*. The fact that we can download many software programs from the internet means that many people no longer pay the licence fee to Microsoft. MP3 enables people to listen to music without paying royalties to the musicians.

MANAGING CHANGE

Perhaps the overriding theme within the business world today is the speed at which change is occurring. The Japanese coined the term *kaizen* to mean 'continuous improvement'; everything that you do can always be improved upon.

The fact that the firm's competitors are constantly improving themselves and that profit margins are getting tighter and tighter means that there is all the more pressure to improve yourself as well otherwise you may go under.

There are whole areas of business management concerned solely with how this change should be implemented. Change can be disruptive and some employees may resist it.

KNOWLEDGE MANAGEMENT

Knowledge management is concerned with the most efficient ways of making information available to everyone who needs to know things, giving each as much as they need without falling into information overload. There is nothing more tedious than a computer printout that tells you everything about every department so that you then have to spend hours extracting the information you actually wanted.

A highly competitive firm should know what resources it has amongst its staff so that is it able to use these to their optimum. For example, they may have a native Spanish speaker whose talents could be invaluable in a certain transaction.

SALARY EXPECTATIONS

Despite the retention problems quoted by employers, statistics show that across the UK the average manager is in his/her early 40s and has been with the organisation for about 14 years. A manager of this age with this amount of experience would be earning around £40,000 per year.

In 2006, the AGR Graduate Recruitment Survey reported that the average graduate starting salary for the 2005/06 recruitment year saw a 2.9% year-on-year increase. The highest paying companies were investment banks and fund managers who paid an average starting salary of £36,000. Management consultants/business services firms offered a median salary of £28,500, accountancy/professional services firms offered £24,500, and banking and financial services offered £22,000 and £18,597 was paid for finance, insurance, pensions and actuarial work.

IMPACT OF TERRORISM

The international threat of terrorism is having an impact on the global economy, but some sectors are feeling the impact more than others. Travel and tour companies have taken the biggest battering to date due, in the short term, to the psychological impact on consumers who are afraid to fly or visit tourist locations in some parts of the world. Stores that have had major outlets in travel hubs such as airports and train stations have also suffered. WHSmith, for example, has seen a fall in share prices and is worried about the effect this will have on trade. Supermarkets, on the other hand are still trading comfortably, as people are feeling safer closer to home and are not neglecting their general routine in the light of heightened terror alerts.

Terrorism can have both a direct and indirect bearing on the economy. Terrorism impacts directly on the economy in the short term when it concerns the damage done to people's lives and property, immediate responses to the emergency and rebuilding the affected systems, buildings and infrastructure. These costs, however, tend to be in proportion to the scale of the attack sustained. The indirect costs of terrorism mean that investors and consumers lose their confidence in the economy. Often strong consumer confidence goes a long way towards boosting an economy, a particular example being the US prior to the 2001 terror attacks, and the economy suffers as this confidence wanes. The threat of terrorism can also potentially negatively affect productivity in the sense that transaction costs might be increased by higher insurance premiums, and counter-terrorism regulations. The impact that terrorism will have on the global economy is being continually assessed and its full impact will depend on how long the campaign against terrorism continues and how quickly consumer confidence can be regained.

EU ENLARGEMENT

May Day 2004 brought about the largest expansion of the European Union in its history: the 15 existing member states were joined by eight former Soviet-bloc countries and two Mediterranean islands, bringing the total membership to 25 countries. The ten new members (Czech Republic, Cyprus, Estonia, Hungary, Latvia, Lithuania, Malta, Poland, Slovakia and Slovenia) became equal members. The sixth stage of enlargement was finalised in January 2007 with the entry of Bulgaria and Romania.

The Balkan countries have been promised entry when they meet the economic conditions and Croatia, Macedonia and Turkey have already been given *candidate status*. EU treaties, however, will have to be revised before any more countries can join as the Treaty of Nice stipulated that 27 members would be the maximum. Experts say the EU may be prepared to 'tinker' with treaties to allow Croatia in, but major reform will be necessary after that.

Joining the European Union does not immediately guarantee economic convergence and it will take some time before per capita GDP of the new member states matches that of the original 15. The new arrivals will have to rely on the other benefits of EU membership. The principal benefits of entry into the European Union beyond political stability and economic openness are not the regional aid they receive but the liberal movements of goods, capital and labour.

Goods and capital can move freely but the free movement of labour has met with some opposition initially. Some in the West object to the influx of masses from the East while some in the East are unhappy about losing their best academics and professionals to the West. Restrictions can potentially be placed on workers from Bulgaria and Romania but cannot be continued for more than seven years. Countries which impose restrictions must inform European Commission why they think the foreign workers would distort their labour market.

It is not difficult to understand why the new members will seem attractive to investors and importers with their cheap labour costs and lower taxes. The benefits may be short-lived, however, as these aspects will undoubtedly change with further integration.

McDonald's

Morgan Spurlock's documentary *Super Size Me* had a huge impact on the image of McDonald's and could be said to have influenced the significant changes that McDonald's have recently made to their menus. Spurlock's experiment consisted of him eating McDonald's meals for breakfast, lunch and dinner every day for thirty days, trying everything on the menu as he did so. At the same time, he minimised the amount of physical exercise he was doing in order to emulate the average American. His audiences were appalled by what they were seeing – witnessing first-hand his body's reactions to this experiment. McDonald's then made some important announcements about changes to their menus. The first to be made was that super-sizing (massive portions of fries and Coke) was to be abolished and that the 'Happy Meal' would become the 'Go Active Happy Meal' complete with salad, free exercise manual and stepometer.

Although these announcements were made shortly after the first showings of the docu-film, McDonald's denied they were made in reaction to it. They had begun developing their 'New Tastes Menu' eighteen months previously. New product ranges included 'Low-fat Chicken Salsa Flatbread', 'Penne Salad' and 'The 80g Happy Meal Fruit Bag'. McDonald's now also provide nutritional information on all products so that customers are aware of the number of calories they are consuming. McDonald's had felt the need to re-invent their image in this way in response to their first ever quarterly loss in 2003. They felt that they had no option but to re-invent their brand after fears of the dangers of obesity and the expansion of consumer choice. Legal action taken by obese children in an attempt to seek damages from McDonald's was thrown out in US courts but it does open up the possibility of litigation in the future.

GROWTH OF CHINA

Businesses have become increasingly international in the last decade and the world has become a smaller place in which to trade. The three regional trading areas – Europe, the Americas and Asia – are all competing for dominance and the dominant partnerships are ever changing. China has proved that it can live up to its potential to perform on the world economic stage: its economy has experienced an incredible boom since the 1990s and rose 10.7% in 2006, reaching an 11-year high. China became a member of the World Trade Organization in 2001 and is currently working on building the instruments and mechanisms needed to float the renminbi currency on the foreign exchange markets. Businesses in the West have had to make radical changes to their structures, systems and working measures to compete with the lower labour costs and flexible manufacturing systems in Asia, and will need to continue this review to stay competitive in the global marketplace.

8

LIST OF DEGREE COURSES

The following pages are designed to give you some crucial, albeit skeletal, information at a glance. They simply list degree-awarding institutions with the names of mainly full-time business and management courses on offer as of November 2006.

Courses are usually three or four years. It is generally four years for courses with study abroad, indicated by (A), and for sandwich degrees with a year in industry, indicated by (S). Depending on the institution and the content of the course of study, the degree qualification may be a BA or a BSc. Honours degrees are indicated by (H). It is important to remember that since degree courses can change format frequently, you must check with universities directly to confirm details. Check with *Trotman's Green Guides: Business Courses*, published annually by Trotman, for a comprehensive listing of business courses.

This table does not include any Foundation degrees. These are generally two-year full-time (or three-year part-time) courses which are offered by universities in partnership with higher education colleges and colleges of further education. If you opt for a Foundation course you can usually complete a top-up year to convert it to a full degree. There are no set entry requirements as it is up to the institution to decide if you are eligible. Work experience can often be more relevant than academic qualifications here. It is best to check with the institution concerned. An additional benefit of these courses is that they tend to give some flexibility about which subjects are taken as part of the programme.

Finding the course that best suits your interests and abilities from the many hundreds on offer can seem like a daunting prospect, but it pays to take time to make the right choice. In Chapter 2, you will find information and advice on how to approach the decision-making process and suggested strategies for creating and narrowing down your shortlist of courses.

For up-to-date information on business and management, go to www.mpw.co.uk/getintobus

University of Abertay Dundee
www.abertay.ac.uk

Business Studies	BA(H)	4y
International Management	BA(H)	4y
Management Studies	BA(H)	4y

Anglia Ruskin University
www.anglia.ac.uk

Business and Law	BA(H)	3y
Business and Social Policy	BA(H)	3y
Business Management	BA(H)	3y
Business with languages (A)	BA(H)/BSc(H)	4y
Business Economics	BA(H)	3y
Business Studies	BA(H)	4y
Corporate Management	BA(H)	3y

Aston University
www.aston.ac.uk

Business Computing and Information Technology (S)	BSc(H)	4y
Business Research and Consultancy	BSc(H)	3y/4y(S)
International Business and Economics (S)	BSc(H)	4y
International Business and Management (S)	BSc(H)	4y

University of Wales, Bangor
www.bangor.ac.uk

Administration and Management	BA(H)	3y
Business and Management	BA(H)	3y
Business and Social Administration	BA(H)	3y
Business Studies and Economics	BA(H)	3y
Business Studies with languages	BA(H)	3y/4y(A)

University of Bath
www.bath.ac.uk

Business Adminstration (S & A)	BSc(H)	4y
International Management and French (S & A)	BSc(H)	4y

International Management and German (S & A)	BSc(H)	4y
International Management and Spanish (S & A)	BSc(H)	4y

Bath Spa University
www.bathspa.ac.uk

Business and Management and options	BA(H)/BSc(H)	3y
Management and options	BA(H)	3y
Tourism Management	BSc(H)	3y

University of Bedfordshire
www.beds.ac.uk

Business Decision Making	BSc(H)	3y
Business Management (A)	BA(H)	3/4y
Business Studies (A)	BA(H)	3/4y
Business Studies with Options (S)	BA(H)	4y

University of Birmingham
www.bham.ac.uk

Business Management (subject to validation)	BA(H)	3y

Birmingham College of Food, Tourism and Creative Studies
www.bcftcs.ac.uk

Events Management (S)	BA(H)	4y
Marketing with Events Management	BA(H)	3y
Marketing with Tourism Management	BA(H)	3y
Marketing Management	BA(H)	3y
Retail Management	BA(H)	3y
Sports Management	BA(H)	3y

University of Bolton
www.bolton.ac.uk

Business Studies	BA(H)	3y
Human Resource Management	BA(H)	3y

Bournemouth University
www.bournemouth.ac.uk

Business Studies (S)	BA(H)	4y
Business Studies with Finance	BA(H)	4y
Retail Management (S)	BA(H)	4y
Tourism Management (S)	BA(H)	4y

University of Bradford
www.brad.ac.uk

Business Studies and Law	BA(H)	3/4y
International Business and Management	BSc(H)	3/4y
Business Studies with Options (S)	BA(H)	4y

Bradford College
www.bradfordcollege.ac.uk

Business Administration	BA(H)	3y
Business and E-Commerce	BA(H)	3y
Business Studies	BA(H)	3y

Bristol, University of the West of England
www.uwe.ac.uk

Business Administration	BA(H)	3y
Business Enterprise (S)	BA(H)	4y
Business Studies with Human Resources Management (S)	BA(H)	4y
Management and Information Systems	BA(H)	4y

Brunel University
www.brunel.ac.uk

Business and Management	BSc(H)	3/4y
Business and Management (Marketing)	BSc(H)	3y
Business and Management (Marketing) (S)	BSc(H)	4y
Business and Management (E-Business Systems)	BSc(H)	3y
Business and Management (E-Business Systems) (S)	BSc(H)	4y
Business and Management (Accounting)	BSc(H)	3y
Business and Management (Accounting) (S)	BSc(H)	4y

Business Studies and Sports Sciences	BSc(H)	3y

University of Buckingham
www.buckingham.ac.uk

Business Studies	BSc(H)	2y

Buckinghamshire Chilterns University College
www.bcuc.ac.uk

Business and Advertising Management	BA(H)	3/4y
Business Management	BA(H)	3/4y
Business Management with Marketing Communications	BA(H)	3/4y
Business Management with Finance	BA(H)	3/4y
Business with Personnel Management	BA(H)	3/4y
Business Management with Law	BA(H)	3/4y
Business Management with Marketing	BA(H)	3/4y
International Management	BA(H)	3y

University of Cambridge
www.cam.ac.uk

Management Studies	BA(H)	1y

Canterbury Christ Church University
www.cant.ac.uk

Business Studies	BA(H)	3y
Business Studies with Options	BA(H)	3y
Business Studies with French	BA(H)/BSc(H)	3y
Business Studies and Marketing	BA(H)/BSc(H)	3y
Business Studies and Media and Cultural Studies	BA(H)/BSc(H)	3y
Business Studies and Music	BA(H)/BSc(H)	3y
Business Studies and Psychology	BA(H)/BSc(H)	3y
Business Studies and Religious Studies	BA(H)/BSc(H)	3y
Business Studies and Sociology	BA(H)/BSc(H)	3y

Cardiff University
www.cardiff.ac.uk

Business Administration with a European Language (A)	BSc(H)	4y
Business Management and options	BSc(H)	3y

University of Wales Institute, Cardiff
www.uwic.ac.uk

International Business Management	BA(H)	3y
Business Studies	BA(H)	3y
Retail Management	BA(H)	3y
Tourism Management	BA(H)	3y
Business Studies and options	BA(H)	3y
Business Studies with languages	BA(H)	3y

Castle College Nottingham
www.peoples.ac.uk

Business Administration	BA(H)	3y

CECOS London College of IT and Management
www.cecos.co.uk

Business and Management Studies	BSc(H)	3y

University of Central Lancashire
www.uclan.ac.uk

Business	BA(H)	3y
Business and options	BA(H)	3y
Management and options	BA(H)	3y

University of Chester
www.chester.ac.uk

Business and options	BA(H)	3y
Management	BA(H)	3y
Management and options	BA(H)	3y
Management with languages	BA(H)	3y
Business with languages	BA(H)	3y
Management with languages	BA(H)	3y
Management with languages	BA(H)	3y

University of Chichester
www.chi.ac.uk

Business Studies	BA(H)	3/4y
Business Studies and options	BA(H)	3/4y
Tourism Management	BA(H)	3/4y

City University
www.city.ac.uk

Management	BSc(H)	3/4y

Colchester Institute
www.colch-inst.ac.uk

Management	BA(H)	3y
Management of Sport	BA(H)	3y
Management of Tourism	BA(H)	3y

Coventry University
www.cov.ac.uk

Business Administration	BA(H)	3y
Business Enterprise	BA(H)	3y
Business Management	BA(H)	3/4y
Business Management	BA(H)	3y
Business and options	BA(H)	3y

Craven College
www.craven-college.ac.uk

Business Management	BA(H)	1y

Croydon College
www.croydon.ac.uk

Business	BA(H)	3y

De Montfort University
www.dmu.ac.uk

Business Studies	BA(H)	3/4y
Business and options	BA(H)	3/4y
E-Business	BA(H)	3/4y

University of Derby
www.derby.ac.uk

Business Studies	BA(H)	3/4y
Enterprise Management and Business Psychology	BA(H)	3y

Enterprise Management and English	BSc(H)	3y
Enterprise Management and Marketing	BSc(H)	3y
Enterprise Management and Website Development	BSc(H)	3y

University of Derby at Buxton
www.derby.ac.uk/buxton

Business Operations Management and Hair Care Management	BA(H)	3y
Business Operations Management and Leisure	BA(H)	3y
Business Operations Management and Spa Management	BA(H)	3y
Culinary Arts and Business Operations Management	BA(H)	3y
Licensed Retail and Business Operations Management	BA(H)	3y

Doncaster College
www.don.ac.uk

Business and Management	BA(H)	3y
Business Studies (S)	BA(H)	4y

University of Dundee
www.dundee.ac.uk

E-Commerce Computing (Business)	BSc(H)	4y
E-Commerce Computing (Business)	BSc(H)	3y

University of Durham
www.dur.ac.uk

Business	BA(H)	3y
Business Finance	BA(H)	3y

University of East Anglia
www.uea.ac.uk

Business Management	BSc(H)	3y

University of East London
www.uel.ac.uk

Business Studies and Education and Community Development	BA(H)	3y
Business Studies and English Language	BA(H)	3y
Business Studies and Law	BA(H)	3y
Business Studies with Marketing for Design	BA(H)	3y
Business Studies with Printed Textile and Surface Decoration	BA(H)	3y
Business Studies and Sociology	BA(H)	3y
Business Studies (Corporate Responsibility) (S)	BA(H)	4y
Business Studies (Entrepreneurship)	BA(H)	3/4y

Edge Hill University
www.edgehill.ac.uk

Business and Management Studies	BSc(H)	3y
Business with Law	BA(H)	3y

University of Essex
www.essex.ac.uk

Business Management	BSc(H)	3y
Financial Management	BSc(H)	3y
Management and Mathematics	BSc(H)	3y
Business Studies with English Language	BA(H)	3y
Management with Leadership	BA(H)	3y
Management with Leadership (with European study) (A)	BA(H)	4y

Farnborough College of Technology
www.farn-ct.ac.uk

Business Management	BA(H)	3y
Business Management with Leisure Management	BA(H)	3y

FTC Kaplan
www.ftckaplan.com

Business Accounting	BA(H)	2y

University of Glamorgan
www.glam.ac.uk

Business Studies	BA(H)	3/4y
Managment and Business	BA(H)	1y

Glasgow Caledonian University
www.gcal.ac.uk

Business Management	BA(H)	4y
Business and Management	BA(H)	4y
Business Information Management	BA(H)	4y

University of Gloucestershire
www.glos.ac.uk

Business Management (S)	BA(H)	4y
Business Management and options	BA(H)/BSc(H)	3y/4y(S)
Management	BA(H)	3y

Greenwich School of Management
www.greenwich-college.ac.uk

Business Management	BSc(H)	2y
Business Management and Information Technology	BSc(H)	2y
Business Management (Travel and Tourism)	BSc(H)	2y

University of Greenwich
www.gre.ac.uk

Tourism Management	BA(H)	3/4y
Business Administration	BA(H)	3y
Business Administration and options	BA(H)/BSc(H)	3y
Business Administration with languages	BA(H)/BSc(H)	3y
Business and options	BA(H)/BSc(H)	3y
Business with languages	BA(H)/BSc(H)	3y
Business Studies with languages	BA(H)/BSc(H)	3y

Grimsby Institute of Further and Higher Education
www.grimsby.ac.uk

Business Management	BA(H)	3y
Tourism and Business Management	BA(H)	3y

Harper Adams University College
www.harper-adams.ac.uk

Business Management with Marketing	BSc/BSc(H)	3y/4y(S)
Tourism and Business Management	BSc/BSc(H)	3y/4y(S)

Hartpury College
www.hartpury.ac.uk

Agricultural Business Management	BA(H)	3y

Heriot-Watt University
www.hw.ac.uk

Business Management (S)	BA(H)	4y

University of Hertfordshire
www.herts.ac.uk

Business Studies (S)	BA(H)	4y
Business and options (A)	BSc(H)	3/4y
Business with languages (A)	BSc(H)	3/4y
Business Administration	BA(H)	3y
Management Science with languages	BSc(H)	3/4y
Management Science and languages	BA(H)/BSc(H)	3y/4y(S)
Management Sciences and options	BA(H)/BSc(H)	3y/4y(S)
Information Systems and Management Science	BA(H)/BSc(H)	3y/4y(S)
International Tourism Management (S)	BA(H)	4y

University of Huddersfield
www.hud.ac.uk

Business and options	BA(H)	3/4y
Business Studies	BA(H)	3/4y

Business Studies with		
Environmental Management	BA(H)	3/4y
Management and Accountancy	BA(H)	3/4y
Retail Management	BA(H)	3/4y

University of Hull
www.hull.ac.uk

Business	BA(H)	3y
Business (International)	BA(H)	4y
Business Management and		
Information Technology	BA(H)	3y
Business and Management		
(International) (A)	BA(H)	4y
Business and Management (S)	BA(H)	4y
Business Management and Information		
Technology (International) (A)	BA(H)	4y
Business Management and		
Information Technology (S)	BA(H)	4y
Business and options	BA(H)	3y
Management and		
Business Economics	BA(H)	3y
Management and Human		
Resource Management	BA(H)	3y
Management and Marketing	BA(H)	3y
Management and Public Relations	BA(H)	3y

Huron University, USA in London
www.huron.ac.uk

Business Administration	BSc(H)	4y

Keele University
www.keele.ac.uk

Business Administration	
and options	BA(H)/BSc(H) 3y/4y(A)
Management Science	
and Mathematics	BA(H)/BSc(H) 3y/4y(A)
Management Science and Media, Communications	
and Culture	BA(H)/BSc(H) 3y/4y(A)
Management Science	
and Music Technology	BA(H)/BSc(H) 3y/4y(A)
Management Science	
and Physics	BA(H)/BSc(H) 3y/4y(A)

Management Science and Psychology	BA(H)/BSc(H)	3y/4y(A)

Kensington College of Business
www.kensingtoncoll.ac.uk

Business Studies	BA(H)	3y

University of Kent
www.kent.ac.uk

Management Science	BSc(H)	3/4y
Management Science with Computing	BSc(H)	3/4y
Tourism Management	BA(H)	3y
Tourism Management (S)	BA(H)	4y

King's College London (University of London)
www.kcl.ac.uk

Business Management	BSc(H)	3y

Kingston University
www.kingston.ac.uk

Business Administration	BA(H)	1y
Business Management	BA(H)	3y
Business Management Analysis	BA(H)/BSc(H)	3y/4y(A)
Business with Law	BA(H)	3y
Business with Law (S)	BA(H)	4y
Business with Law (A)	BA(H)	4y
Entrepreneurship and Management	BA(H)	3y
Entrepreneurship and Management (S)	BA(H)	4y

Kingston College
www.kingston-college.ac.uk

Business Management	BA(H)	3y

University of Wales, Lampeter
www.lamp.ac.uk

Business Management	BA(H)	3y
Business Management and options (A)	BA(H)	3/4y

Lancaster University
www.lancs.ac.uk

Business Studies	BSc(H)	3y
Management and Entrepreneurship (S)	BA(H)	4y
Management and Organisation (Human Resource Management) (S)	BA(H)	4y
Management and Organisation (A)	BA(H)	3y
Management Science (A)	BSc(H)	3y
Business Studies	BSc(H)	3y
Management Science	BSc(H)	3/4y

University of Leeds
www.leeds.ac.uk

Accounting and Management	BA(H)	3y/4y(A/S)
Economics and Management	BA(H)	3y
Management	BA(H)	3y/4y(A/S)
Management Studies and languages	BA(H)	3y/4y(A)
Management Studies and Law	BA(H)	4y
Management Studies and Mathematics	BSc(H)	3y/4y(A/S)
Management Studies and Pharmacology	BSc(H)	3y/4y(A/S)
Management Studies and Philosophy	BA(H)	3y
Management Studies and Psychology	BA(H)	3y

Leeds Metropolitan University
www.leedsmet.ac.uk

Business and Human Resource Management	BA(H)	3/4y
Business and Management	BA(H)	3/4y
Project Management	BSc(H)	3/4y
Retail Marketing Management	BA(H)	3/4y
Sales Management	BA(H)	3/4y

Leeds Trinity & All Saints
www.leedstrinity.ac.uk

Business	BA(H)	3y

Business and Law	BA(H)	3y
Business and Management	BA(H)	3y
Business and Marketing	BA(H)	3y
Business and Sport/Leisure	BA(H)	3y
Management	BA(H)	3y

University of Leicester
www.le.ac.uk

Management Studies	BA(H)	3y

Lisburn Institute of Further and Higher Education
www.liscol.ac.uk

Business Studies	BA(H)	1y

Liverpool Hope University
www.hope.ac.uk

Business and options	BA(H)/BSc(H)	3y
Business Studies	BA(H)	3y

Liverpool John Moores University
www.ljmu.ac.uk

Business and Economics	BA(H)	3/4y
Business and Finance	BA(H)	3y
Business and Public Relations (S)	BA(H)	3/4y
Business Management	BA(H)	3y
Business Management and Information	BA(H)	3y
Business Mathematics (S)	BSc/BSc(H)	4y
Business Studies (S)	BA(H)	3/4y

University of Liverpool
www.liv.ac.uk

Business Studies	BA(H)	3/4y
Business Studies and French (A)	BA(H)	4y
Business Studies and German	BA(H)	4y
Business Studies and Hispanic Studies (A)	BA(H)	4y
Business Studies and Italian	BA(H)	3y
Legal and Business Studies	BA(H)	3y

London Academy of Administrative Studies
www.london-academy.com

Business Administration	BSc	3y

London College of Communication, University of the Arts London
www.lcc.arts.ac.uk

Retail Management	BA(H)	3y

London College, UCK
www.lcuck.ac.uk

Business Studies	BSc	3y

London International College
www.londonic.org.uk

Business Management	BSc	3y

London Metropolitan University
www.londonmet.ac.uk

Business Administration	BA(H)	3y
Business Enterprise	BA(H)	3y
Business Studies (S)	BA(H)	4y
Business and options	BA(H)/BSc(H)	3y/4y(A)
Management and Public Administration	BA(H)/BSc(H)	3y/4y(A)

London School of Commerce
www.lsclondon.co.uk

Business Studies	BA(H)	3y

London School of Economics and Political Science, University of London
www.lse.ac.uk

Management	BSc(H)	3y
Management Sciences	BSc(H)	3y

London School of Science and Technology
www.lsst.com

Management and Information Systems	BSc(H)	3y

London South Bank University
www.lsbu.ac.uk

Business Administration	BA(H)	3y
Business Studies (S)	BA(H)	4y
Management and Marketing	BA(H)/BSc(H)	3y/4y(A)
Management and Media Studies	BA(H)/BSc(H)	3y/4y(A)
Management and Psychology	BA(H)/BSc(H)	3y/4y(A)
Management and Social Policy	BA(H)/BSc(H)	3y/4y(A)
Management and Sociology	BA(H)/BSc(H)	3y/4y(A)

Loughborough University
www.lboro.ac.uk

Retail Management (S)	BSc(H)	4y

LVMT Business School
www.lvmt.com

Business	BSc	2/3y
Management	BSc	2/3y

University of Manchester
www.manchester.ac.uk

Business Management with languages (A)	BA(H)	4y
International Management (A)	BSc(H)	4y
International Management with American Business Studies (A)	BSc(H)	4y
International Management with French (A)	BSc(H)	4y
Management	BSc(H)	3y
Management with Options	BSc(H)	3y

Manchester Metropolitan University
www.mmu.ac.uk

Business Administration (with options in named pathways)	BA(H)	1y
Business in Europe (French route) (A)	BA(H)	4y
Business in Europe (German route) (A)	BA(H)	4y

Business in Europe (Italian route) (A)	BA(H)	4y
Business in Europe (Spanish route) (A)	BA(H)	4y
Business (with options in named pathways) (S)	BA(H)	4y
Business Management	BA(H)	3y
Business and options	BA(H)/BSc(H)	3y

Mid-Kent College of Higher and Further Education
www.midkent.ac.uk

Business Studies (S)	BA(H)	4y
Tourism Management	BA(H)	3/4y

Middlesex University
www.mdx.ac.uk

Business Administration (A)	BA(H)	3y
Business Analysis	BSc(H)	3/4y
Business Information Systems and Management	BSc	3/4y
Business Analysis	BSc(H)	3/4y
Business Studies with options	BA(H)/BSc/BSc(H)	3y
International Management	BA(H)	3/4y
Management and options	BA(H)/BSc/BSc(H)	3y
Management with languages	BA(H)/BSc/BSc(H)	3y

Napier University
www.napier.ac.uk

Business Studies	BA(H)	4y/5y (S)
Business Studies and Psychology	BA(H)	3/4y
Business Studies and options	BA(H)	4/5y
Tourism Management (S)	BA(H)	4y

New College Durham
www.newdur.ac.uk

Management, Business and Administration	BA(H)	1y

Newcastle University
www.ncl.ac.uk

Economics and Business Management (S)	BA(H)	4y
Farm Business Management	BSc(H)	3y

Newcastle College
www.newcastlecollege.co.uk

Public Service Management	BA(H)	1y

Newman College of Higher Education
www.newman.ac.uk

Management Studies and options	BA(H)	3y

University of Wales, Newport
www.newport.ac.uk

Business and options	BSc(H)	3y
E-Business Management	BSc(H)	3y

North East Wales Institute of Higher Education
www.newi.ac.uk

Business Accounting	BA(H)	3y
Business Management	BA(H)	3y
Business Management and options	BA(H)	3y

North West Kent College
www.nwkcollege.ac.uk

Business Administration	BA(H)	3y

University of Northampton
www.northampton.ac.uk

Business Entrepreneurship	BA(H)	3y
Business Studies	BA(H)	3/4y
Business and options	BA(H)/BSc(H)	3y
Management and options	BA(H)/BSc(H)	3y
Management with languages	BA(H)/BSc(H)	3y

Northbrook College Sussex
www.northbrook.ac.uk

Business Administration	BA(H)	3y

Northumbria University
www.northumbria.ac.uk

Advertising Management (S)	BA(H)	4y
Business and options	BA(H)	3/4y
Business Studies (S)	BA(H)	4y
International Business Administration (A)	BA(H)	4y
International Business Management (A)	BA(H)	4y

City College Norwich
www.ccn.ac.uk

Business Management	BA(H)	3y

University of Nottingham
www.nottingham.ac.uk

Management Studies	BA(H)	3y
Management Studies with languages (A)	BA(H)	4y
Management with Asian Studies	BA(H)	3y
Management with Chinese Studies	BA(H)	3y

Nottingham Trent University
www.ntu.ac.uk

Business, Information Communications Technology and Education	BSc(H)	3y
Business and Computing for Sciences	BSc(H)	3y
Business and Educational Development	BA(H)	3y
Business and Information Systems	BA(H)	3y
International Management (in-company)	BA(H)	3y

University Centre Oldham
www.oldham.hud.ac.uk

Business Management	BA(H)	3y

Open University

www.open.ac.uk

Business Studies	BA(H)	5/6y
Business Studies with Accounting	BA(H)	5/6y
Business Studies with Economics	BA(H)	5/6y
Business Studies with French	BA(H)	5/6y
Business Studies with Information and Communication Technology	BA(H)	5/6y
Business Studies with Law	BA(H)	5/6y
Business Studies with Spanish	BA(H)	5/6y
Business Studies with Systems Practice	BA(H)	5/6y
Business Studies	BA(H)	5/6y
Computing with Business	BSc(H)	5/6y

University of Oxford

www.ox.ac.uk

Economics and Management	BA(H)	3y

Oxford Brookes University

www.brookes.ac.uk

Business Information Systems	BA(H)	3/4y
Business Innovation and Enterprise	BA(H)	3/4y
Business Logistics	BA(H)	3/4y
Business and options	BA(H)	3/4y
Human Resource Management and Business	BSc(H)	3/4y
International Business Management	BA(H)	3/4y
Marketing Management	BA(H)	3y
Retail and Business Management	BA(H)	3/4y

University of Paisley

www.paisley.ac.uk

Business	BA(H)	4/5y
Business Analysis	BA(H)	4/5y
Business Information Technology with options	BA(H)	4/5y
Management	BA(H)	4/5y

Peterborough Regional College

www.peterborough.ac.uk

Business, Management and Organisation	BA(H)	3y
Combined Studies (Business and Law)	BSc(H)	3y
Combined Studies (Business and Social Sciences)	BSc(H)	3y

University of Plymouth

www.plymouth.ac.uk

Business Administration	BA(H)	3/4y
Business Management with Business English	BA(H)	3y
Business Studies (S)	BA(H)	4y
Business and Tourism	BSc(H)	3/4y
Decision Analysis and Business	BSc(H)	3y
International Tourism Management	BSc(H)	3/4y
Tourism Management	BSc(H)	3/4y

University of Portsmouth

www.port.ac.uk

Business Administration	BA(H)	3y
Business Enterprise Development (S)	BA(H)	4y
Business Studies (S)	BA(H)	4y
Enterprise in E-Business	BA(H)	3/4y
Enterprise in Product Design	BSc(H)	3/4y

Queen Margaret University College, Edinburgh

www.qmuc.ac.uk

Business Management	BA(H)	4y
Consumer Studies and Management	BA(H)	4y
Consumer Studies and Retailing	BA(H)	4y
Management and Marketing	BA(H)	4y
Management and Sociology	BA(H)	4y

Queen Mary, University of London

www.qmul.ac.uk

Business Computing		
with Management	BSc	3y
Business Management	BSc(H)	3y

Queen's University Belfast

www.qub.ac.uk

Management	BSc(H)	3y
Management and		
Information Systems	BSc(H)	3y
Management with French (A)	BSc(H)	4y
Management with German (A)	BSc(H)	4y

University of Reading

www.rdg.ac.uk

Business Analysis	BA(H)	3y
International Management and Business Administration		
with French (A)	BA(H)	4y
International Management and Business Administration		
with German (A)	BA(H)	4y
International Management and Business Administration		
with Italian (A)	BA(H)	4y
Management and		
Business Administration	BA(H)	3y
Management with		
Information Technology	BSc(H)	4y

Richmond, the American International University in London

www.richmond.ac.uk

Business Administration (Finance)	BA(H)	3/4y
Business Administration		
(International Business)	BA(H)	3/4y
Business Administration		
(Marketing)	BA(H)	3/4y

Robert Gordon University

www.rgu.ac.uk

Management	BA(H)	3/4y
Management with Economics (S)	BA(H)	4y
Management with Finance (S)	BA(H)	4y

Management with Human		
Resource Management (S)	BA(H)	3/4y
Management with Marketing (S)	BA(H)	4y
Retail Management	BA(H)	4y

Roehampton University
www.roehampton.ac.uk

Business Management	BSc(H)	3y
Business Studies	BSc(H)	3y
Business Studies and options	BA(H)/BSc(H)	3y/4y(A)
Business Studies with languages	BA(H)/BSc(H)	3y/4y(A)
Retail Management and Marketing	BA(H)	3y

Royal Holloway, University of London
www.rhul.ac.uk

Economics and Management	BSc(H)	3y
Management	BSc(H)	3y
Management and Information Systems	BSc(H)	3/4y
Management and options	BA(H)/BSc(H)	3y/4y(A)
Management with languages	BA(H)/BSc(H)	3y/4y(A)

University of St Andrews
www.st-and.ac.uk

Management	BSc(H)	4y
Management Science	BSc(H)	4y
Management with French	BSc(H)	4y
Management with French (A)	BSc(H)	5y
Management with Spanish	BSc(H)	4y
Management with Spanish (A)	BSc(H)	5y

College of St Mark & St John
www.marjon.ac.uk

Management and options	BA(H)	3y

St Martin's College
www.ucsm.ac.uk

Business and Human Resources	BA(H)	3y
Business and Information Technology	BA(H)	3y

Business and Management Studies	BA(H)	3y
Business and Management Studies and Information Technology	BA(H)	3y
Business with Marketing	BA(H)	3y

St Mary's College
www.smuc.ac.uk

Management	BA(H)	3y
Management Studies and options	BA(H)/BSc(H)	3y
Tourism Management	BA(H)	3y

University of Salford
www.salford.ac.uk

Business Decision Analysis	BSc(H)	3/4y
Business Decision and Analysis (A)	BSc(H)	3/4y
Management Science	BSc(H)	3/4y
Management Science (A)	BSc(H)	3/4y
Management Science and Information Systems	BSc(H)	3/4y
Management Science and Information Systems (A)	BSc(H)	3/4y
Business Studies with Financial Management	BSc(H)	3/4y
Business Studies with Human Resource Management	BSc(H)	3/4y
Business Studies with International Business Management	BSc(H)	3/4y
Business Studies with Marketing Management	BSc(H)	3/4y
Business Studies with Quantitative Business Management	BSc(H)	3/4y
Business Studies with Service Sector Management	BSc(H)	3/4y
Management with languages (A)	BSc(H)	4y

School of Oriental and African Studies, University of London
www.soas.ac.uk

Management with languages	BA(H)	3/4y
Management and South East Asian Studies	BA(H)	3/4y

Scottish Agricultural College
www.sac.ac.uk

Rural Business Management	BA(H)	4y
Rural Business Management (Agriculture)	BA(H)	4y
Rural Business Management (Environment)	BA(H)	4y
Rural Business Management (Equine)	BA(H)	4y
Rural Business Management (Food Technology)	BA(H)	4y
Rural Business Management (Leisure)	BA(H)	4y

University of Sheffield
www.sheffield.ac.uk

Management	BA(H)	3y
Management and Economics	BA(H)	3y
Management and Japanese Studies (A)	BA(H)	4y
Management and Mathematics	BA(H)	3y

Sheffield Hallam University
www.shu.ac.uk

Business and Accounting	BA(H)	3/4y
Business and Enterprise Management	BA(H)	3/4y
Business and Finance	BA(H)	1y
Business and Financial Management	BA(H)	3/4y
Business and Financial Services (S)	BA(H)	4y
Business and Human Resource Management (S)	BA(H)	4y
Business and Marketing (S)	BA(H)	4y
Business and Technology (S)	BSc(Hons)	4y
Business Modelling and Management (S)	BSc(H)	4y
Information Technology Management (S)	BSc(H)	4y
Business Studies (S)	BA(H)	4y

Solihull College
www.solihull.ac.uk

Business and Management	BA(H)	3y

South East Essex College
www.southend.ac.uk

Business Studies	BA(H)	3y

University of Southampton
www.soton.ac.uk

Management with Entrepreneurship	BSc	3y

Southampton Solent University
www.solent.ac.uk

Business Management	BA(H)	3y
Business and options	BA(H)	3y
Business Studies (S)	BA(H)	4y
Business with Entrepreneurship	BA(H)	3y
Human Resource Management with Management of Change	BA(H)	3y
Human Resource Management with Business Psychology	BA(H)	3y
International Business Management (A)	BA(H)	3y
International Marketing Management	BA(H)	3y
International Tourism Management (A)	BA(H)	3y

Staffordshire University
www.staffs.ac.uk

Business Decision Analysis	BSc(H)	3/4y
Business and options	BA(H)/BSc/BSc(H)	3y
Business Management	BSc(H)	3/4y
Business Management and Computing	BA(H)	3/4y
Business Management and Entrepreneurship	BA(H)	3/4y
Business Studies	BA(H)	3/4y
International Business Management	BA(H)	3/4y
Sustainable Business Management	BA(H)	3/4y

University of Stirling
www.stir.ac.uk

Business Studies	BA(H)	4y
Business Studies and options	BSc/BSc(H)	3y/4y
Business Studies and options	BA(H)	4y
Business Studies with languages	BA(H)	4y
Management Science	BSc/BSc(H)	3y/4y
Management Science and French Language	BSc/BSc(H)	3y/4y
International Management and Intercultural Studies	BA(H)	4y
International Tourism Management	BA(H)	4y
International Management and Intercultural Studies	BA(H)	4y
International Management Studies with European Languages and Society	BA(H)	4y
Tourism Management	BA(H)	4y

University Campus Suffolk
www.ucs.ac.uk

Business Management	BA(H)	3y
Business Management and options	BA(H)	3y

University of Sunderland
www.sunderland.ac.uk

Business Administration	BA(H)	3y
Business Enterprise	BA(H)	3/4y
Business Enterprise and options	BA(H)/BSc(H)	3y/4y(A)
Business and Human Resource Management	BA(H)	3/4y
Business and Management (Enterprise Management)	BA(H)	3/4y
Business and Management (Managing the Business)	BA(H)	3/4y
Business and Management (Marketing Management)	BA(H)	3/4y
Business Management	BA(H)	3/4y
Business Studies (S)	BA(H)	4y
Business Studies and options	BA(H)/BSc(H)	3y/4y(A)
Management with options	BA(H)/BSc(H)	3y/4y(A)

University of Surrey

www.surrey.ac.uk

Business and Management	BSc(H)	3y
Business Management	BSc(H)	3/4y
Business Management and French (S)	BSc(H)	4y
Mathematics with Business Studies (S)	BSc(H)	4y
Retail Management (S)	BSc(H)	4y
Tourism Management	BSc(H)	3/4y

Swansea Institute of Higher Education

www.sihe.ac.uk

Business Studies	BA(H)	3/4y
Business and Finance	BA(H)	3/4y
Business with Psychology	BA(H)	3y
Management	BA(H)	3y
Management with Economics	BA(H)	3y
Management with Retailing	BA(H)	3y
Marketing with Sales Management	BA(H)	3y
Tourism Management	BA(H)	3y

University of Wales, Swansea

www.swan.ac.uk

Business Management	BA(H)/BSc(H)	3y
Business Management and options	BSc(H)	3y
International Business Administration (Australasia)	BA(H)	4y
International Business Administration (Europe) (A)	BA(H)	4y
International Business Administration (Language) (A)	BA(H)	4y
International Business Administration (North America) (A)	BA(H)	4y
International Business Management (Europe) (A)	BSc(H)	4y
International Business Management (Language) (A)	BSc(H)	4y
International Business Management (North America) (A)	BSc(H)	4y

International Management Science (Australasia) (A)	BSc(H)	4y
International Management Science (North America) (A)	BSc(H)	4y
International Management Science (Europe) (A)	BSc(H)	4y
International Management Science (Language) (A)	BSc(H)	4y
International Management Science (North America) (A)	BSc(H)	4y
Management Science	BSc(H)	3y
Management Science (Accounting)	BSc	3y
Management Science (Finance)	BSc	3y
Management Science (Marketing)	BSc(H)	3y
Management Science (Mathematics)	BSc(H)	3y

University of Teesside
www.tees.ac.uk

Business Information Systems	BSc(H)	3/4y
Business Management	BA(H)	3/4y
Business Studies	BA(H)	3/4y
Business Studies with Law	BA(H)	3/4y
Marketing and Retail Management	BA(H)	3/4y
Tourism Management	BA(H)	3/4y

Thames College of Professional Studies
www.tcps.co.uk

Information Systems and Management	BSc	3y

Thames Valley University
www.tvu.ac.uk

Business Studies	BA(H)	3/4y
Business Studies with Human Resource Management	BA(H)	3/4y
Business Studies with Information Systems	BA(H)	3y
Business Studies with Marketing	BA(H)	3/4y
Business Travel and Tourism	BA(H)	3/4y
Marketing with Business	BA(H)	3y

Trinity College Carmarthen
www.trinity-cm.ac.uk

Business Studies and Sports Studies	BA(H)	3y
Business Studies and Tourism	BA(H)	3y
Information Technology with Management	BSc(H)	3y

UCE Birmingham
www.uce.ac.uk

Advertising and Management (S)	BA(H)	3/4y
Business and options	BA(H)	3/4y
Business Psychology and options	BA(H)	3/4y
Business Studies	BA(H)	3/4y
Management and options	BA(H)	3/4y
Marketing and Management	BA(H)	3/4y
Public Relations and Management	BA(H)	3/4y

University College London, University of London
www.ucl.ac.uk

Economics and Business with East European Studies (A)	BA(H)	3y

University of Ulster
www.ulst.ac.uk

Business	BSc(H)	3/4y
Business and options	BSc(H)	3/4y
Business with languages	BSc(H)	3/4y
Business Finance and Investment	BSc(H)	3/4y
Business Studies	BSc(H)	3y/4y(A)
Business Studies and options (S)	BSc(H)	4y
Business Studies with languages (S)	BSc(H)	4y

University of Warwick
www.warwick.ac.uk

Management	BSc(H)	3y

West Kent College
www.wkc.ac.uk

Business Administration (with Marketing, Finance or Human Resource Management)	BA(H)	3y
Tourism Management	BA(H)	3y

University of Westminster
www.wmin.ac.uk

Business	BA(H)	3y
Business (Financial Management)	BA(H)	3y
Business (Human Resource Management)	BA(H)	3y
Business (Information Management)	BA(H)	3y
Business (Marketing)	BA(H)	3y
Business with Property	BA(H)	3y
Business Management	BA(H)	3y
Business Studies (S)	BA(H)	4y
Business Studies and options	BA(H)	4y
European Management (A)	BA(H)	4y
International Business (S)	BA(H)	4y
Information Systems with Business Management (S)	BSc(H)	4y

University of Winchester
www.winchester.ac.uk

Business Management	BA(H)	3y
Business Management with options	BA(H)	3y
Tourism Management	BA(H)	3y

University of Wolverhampton
www.wlv.ac.uk

Business and options	BA(H)/BSc(H)	3/4y
Business and languages	BA(H)/BSc(H)	3/4y
Business Information Systems	BSc(H)	3/4y
Business Management	BA(H)	3y
Business Studies (S)	BA(H)	4y
International Business Management	BA(H)	3/4y

University of Worcester
www.worc.ac.uk

Business Management	BA(H)	3y
Business Management (Finance and Accounting)	BA(H)	3y
Business Management (Global Economy)	BA(H)	3y

Business Management (Human Resources)	BA(H)	3y
Business Management (Marketing)	BA(H)	3y

Writtle College
www.writtle.ac.uk

Business Management	BA(H)	3y

Yeovil College
www.yeovil-college.ac.uk

Business and Management	BA(H)	1y

University of York
www.york.ac.uk

Management	BA(H)/BSc(H)	3y
Management with Information Technology	BA(H)/BSc(H)	3y

York St John University College
www.yorksj.ac.uk

Business Management	BA(H)	3y
Business Management and Finance	BA(H)	3y
Business Management Human Resource Management	BA(H)	3y
Business Management Information Technology	BA(H)	3y
Business Management and Marketing	BA(H)	3y
Business Management and Sports Studies	BA(H)/BSc(H)	3y
Business Management and Theology and Religious Studies	BA(H)/BSc(H)	3y
Business Management and Tourism	BA(H)	3y

9

FURTHER INFORMATION

USEFUL ADDRESSES

Association of Chartered Certified Accountants (ACCA)
29 Lincoln's Inn Fields
London WC2A 3EE
020 7396 5700
www.acca.org.uk

British Chambers of Commerce
65 Petty France
London SW1H 9EU
020 7654 5800
www.chamberonline.co.uk

Chartered Institute of Logistics and Transport
11–12 Buckingham Gate
London SW1E 6LB
01536 740100
www.ciltuk.org.uk

Chartered Institute of Management Accountants
26 Chapter Street
London SW1P 4NP
020 8849 2251
www.cimaglobal.com

Chartered Institute of Marketing
Moor Hall
Cookham
Berkshire SL6 9QH
01628 427500
www.cim.co.uk

Chartered Institute of Personnel and Development
CIPD House
Camp Road
London SW19 4UX
020 8971 9000
www.ipd.co.uk

Chartered Institute of Purchasing and Supply
Easton House
Easton on the Hill
Stamford
Lincolnshire PE9 3NZ
01780 756777
www.cips.org

Chartered Management Institute
3rd Floor
2 Savoy Court, Strand
London WC2R 0EZ
020 7497 0580
www.managers.org.uk

Confederation of British Industry
Centrepoint
103 New Oxford Street
London WC1A 1DU
020 7379 7400
www.cbi.org.uk

Development for Employment and Learning of Northern Ireland
Adelaide House
39–49 Adelaide Street
Belfast BT2 8FD
028 9025 7777
www.delni.gov.uk

Federation of Small Businesses
Sir Frank Whittle Way
Blackpool Business Park
Blackpool
Lancs FY4 2FE
01253 336000
www.fsb.org.uk

Freight Transport Association
Hermes House
St Johns Road
Tunbridge Wells TN4 9UZ
01892 526171
www.fta.co.uk

Higher Education Funding Council for England
External Relations Department
Northavon House
Coldharbour Lane
Bristol BS16 1QD
0117 931 7317
www.hefce.ac.uk

Higher Education Funding Council for Wales
Linden Court
Ilex Close
Llanishen
Cardiff CF14 5DZ
029 2076 1861
www.hefcw.ac.uk

Institute of Administrative Management
Caroline House
55–57 High Holborn
London WC1V 6DX
0207 841 1100
www.instam.org

Institute of Chartered Secretaries and Administrators
16 Park Crescent
London W1B 1BA
020 7580 4741
www.icsa.org.uk

Institute of Credit Management

The Water Mill
Station Road
South Luffenham
Oakham
Leicestershire LE15 8NB
01780 722900
www.icm.org.uk

Institute of Management Consultancy

3rd Floor
17–18 Hayward's Place
London EC1R 0EG
020 7566 5220
www.imc.co.uk

Institute of Management Foundation

Management House
Cottingham Road
Corby
Northants NN17 1TT
01536 204222

Institute of Management Services

Brooke House
24 Dam Street
Lichfield
Staffordshire WS13 6AB
01543 266909
www.ims-productivity.com

Institute of Packaging

Springfield House
Springfield Business Park
Grantham
Lincolnshire NG31 7BG
01476 514590
www.pi2.org.uk

Institute of Quality Assurance

12 Grosvenor Crescent
London SW1X 7EE
020 7245 6722
www.iqa.org

Management Consultancies Association
60 Trafalgar Square
London WC2N 5DS
020 7321 3990
www.mca.org.uk

Operational Research Society
Seymour House
12 Edward Street
Birmingham B1 2RX
0121 233 9300
www.orsoc.org.uk

Prince's Trust
18 Park Square East
London NW1 4LH
020 7543 1234
www.princes-trust.org.uk

Scottish Funding Council
Donaldson House
97 Haymarket Terrace
Edinburgh EH12 5HD
0131 313 6500
www.sfc.ac.uk

Work Foundation
Peter Runge House
3 Carlton House Terrace
London SW1Y 5DG
020 7004 7200
www.theworkfoundation.com

BOOKS

GENERAL HIGHER EDUCATION

Cassell Careers Encyclopedia, Audrey Segal & Katherine Lea,
   Cassell Educational
Choosing Your Degree Course & University, Brian Heap,
   Trotman
Degree Course Offers, Brian Heap, Trotman
Getting into Oxford and Cambridge, Trotman
How to Complete Your UCAS Application, Trotman
Making the Most of University, Trotman
Mature Students' Directory, Trotman
The Potter Guide to Higher Education, Dalebank Books

Student Book, Trotman

The Student Survival Guide, Edwin H Cox and Penelope Hedge

Students' Money Matters, Gwenda Thomas, Trotman

Taking a Year Off, Margaret Flynn, Trotman

The Ultimate University Ranking Guide, Trotman

University and College Entrance: The Official Guide, UCAS

BUSINESS AND MANAGEMENT

The Art of Managing, Bill Scott & Sven Soderberg, Gower

Business: The Ultimate Resource, produced by the Chartered Management Institute

Complete Small Business Guide, Colin Barrow, BBC Publications

Corporate Strategy, Igor Ansoff, Penguin

CRAC Degree Course Guides: Business and Economics, Trotman

The Elephant and the Flea, Charles Handy, Hutchinson

The Empty Raincoat, Charles Handy, Arrow

The Essential Drucker: The Best of Sixty Years of Peter Drucker's Essential Writing on Management, Peter Drucker, HarperCollins

Essential Manager's Manual, Robert Heller and Tim Hindle, Dorling Kindersley

Executive Programmes Casebook, Hobsons, www.exec.hobsons.com

The Future of Money, B. Lietaer, Century/Random House

GET (Graduate Employment and Training), Hobsons plc

Getting into the City, Neil Harris, Trotman

Getting into Financial Services, Neil Harris, Trotman

Goal-Directed Project Management, E Anderson, Kogan Page

Guide to Business Schools, Association of MBAs/Pitman

A Handbook of Management Techniques, M Armstrong, Kogan Page

How Britain's Bosses are Failing You, Roger Trapp, Capstone

Innovation and Entrepreneurship, Peter Drucker, Butterworth Heinemann

Leading Change, John P Kotter, Harvard Business School Press

Making it Happen: Reflections on Leadership, Sir John Harvey Jones, HarperCollins

Making Managers, Charles Handy, Colin Gordon & Colin Randleson

Management Casebook, Hobsons

Managing People, R Thomson, The Institute of Management

Marketing Today, G Oliver, Prentice Hall

MBA Casebook, Hobsons, www.mba.hobsons.com

The Microsoft File, Wendy Goldman Rohm, Times Books

No Logo, Naomi Klein, Flamingo

The One Minute Manager, Kenneth Blanchard & Spencer Johnson, Fontana

Open Society: Reforming Global Capitalism, George Soros, Little, Brown

Open World: The Truth about Globalisation, Philippe Legrain, Abacus

Personnel Management: A New Approach, D Torrington, Prentice Hall

Prospects series, Central Services Unit (CSU) Publications

Psychology at Work, P B Warr, Penguin

Quantitative Approaches in Business Studies, C Morris, Pitman

The Return of Cosmopolitan Capital, Nigel Harris, IB Tauris

The Road Ahead, Bill Gates, Penguin

Thriving on Chaos: Handbook for a Management Revolution, Tom Peters, SOS Free Stock

Trotman's Green Guides: Business Courses, Trotman

The Truth about Markets, John Kay, Penguin

Understanding Organisations, Charles Handy, Penguin

What they Don't Teach you at Harvard Business School, Mark McCormack, Fontana/Collins

Which MBA?, George Bickerstaffe, Prentice Hall